W9-AUJ-943

STRONGHOLDS
AND
SANCTUARIES

The Borderland of England and Wales

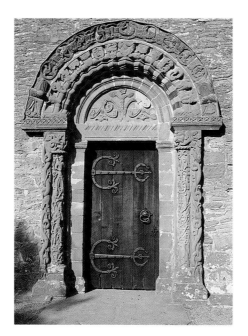

STRONGHOLDS
AND
SANCTUARIES
The Borderland of England and Wales

ELLIS PETERS AND ROY MORGAN

ALAN SUTTON

First published in the United Kingdom in 1993

Alan Sutton Publishing Ltd

Phoenix Mill · Far Thrupp · Stroud · Gloucestershire

First published in the United States of America in 1993

Alan Sutton Publishing Inc.

83 Washington Street · Dover · NH 03820

British Library Cataloguing in Publication Data

Peters, Ellis
  Strongholds and Sanctuaries: Borderland
  of England and Wales
  I. Title
  942

ISBN (hardback) 0–7509–0200–0

ISBN (paperback) 0–7509–0402–X

Library of Congress Cataloging-in-Publication Data applied for

Half-title page photograph: *The south door of Kilpeck church is probably the best preserved carved doorway in England. In this twelfth-century work the outer arches represent creation. The tympanum depicts the 'Tree of Life'.*

Frontispiece photograph: *Edward I built a series of castles (known as the Edwardian Castles) during his conquest of North Wales. Flint Castle was the first: started in 1277 it was complete by 1282.*

Typeset in 11/16 Perpetua.

Typesetting and origination by

Alan Sutton Publishing Limited.

Colour separation by Yeo Valley Graphics.

Printed and bound in Great Britain by

Butler & Tanner Ltd, Frome and London.

Contents

The Norman font of Hereford
Cathedral, about 1150.

The keep of Longtown Castle was built about 1200 with walls 4 metres thick. There was originally a series of outer defences extending over an area of 1.5 hectares.

Acknowledgements

The excerpts from *The Dragon at Noonday, The Hounds of Sunset, Afterglow and Nightfall*, and *A Bloody Field by Shrewsbury*, by Edith Pargeter, are used by kind consent of the publishers, Headline Book Publishing, plc.

Those from *The Green Branch* and *The Marriage of Meggotta*, by Edith Pargeter, are used by kind consent of Little, Brown, publishers.

The Heretic's Apprentice, by Ellis Peters, is a publication of both houses, and I am grateful for their consent to quote from it.

The colours of nature in the Valley of the Cross (Valle Crucis) near Llangollen.

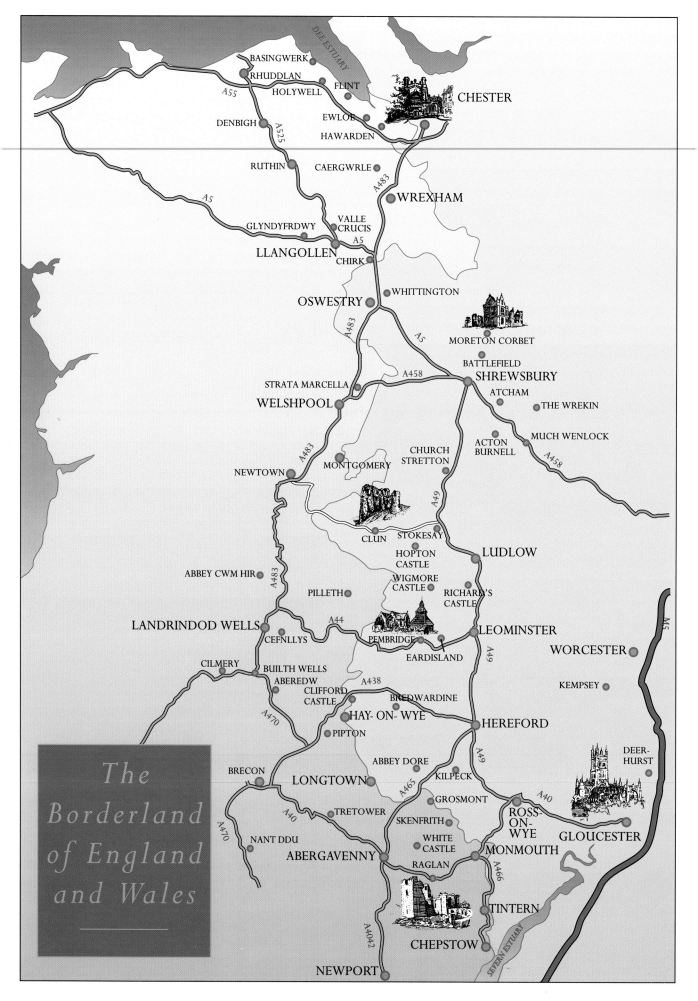

BASINGWERK
RHUDDLAN
FLINT
HOLYWELL
CHESTER
EWLOE
DENBIGH
HAWARDEN
RUTHIN
CAERGWRLE
A55
A525
A483
WREXHAM
A5
GLYNDYFRDWY
VALLE CRUCIS
LLANGOLLEN
A5
CHIRK
OSWESTRY
WHITTINGTON
A483
MORETON CORBET
A5
BATTLEFIELD
STRATA MARCELLA
A458
SHREWSBURY
WELSHPOOL
ATCHAM
THE WREKIN
ACTON BURNELL
MUCH WENLOCK
A458
A483
CHURCH STRETTON
MONTGOMERY
NEWTOWN
A49
CLUN
STOKESAY
LUDLOW
HOPTON CASTLE
ABBEY CWM HIR
WIGMORE CASTLE
A483
PILLETH
RICHARD'S CASTLE
LANDRINDOD WELLS
A44
LEOMINSTER
CEFNLLYS
PEMBRIDGE
WORCESTER
CILMERY
EARDISLAND
A49
BUILTH WELLS
KEMPSEY
ABEREDW
A438
CLIFFORD CASTLE
BREDWARDINE
A470
HAY-ON-WYE
HEREFORD
PIPTON
DEER-HURST
ABBEY DORE
A49
BRECON
LONGTOWN
KILPECK
A465
GROSMONT
A470
TRETOWER
ROSS-ON-WYE
A40
A40
SKENFRITH
GLOUCESTER
NANT DDU
WHITE CASTLE
MONMOUTH
ABERGAVENNY
RAGLAN
A466
A4042
TINTERN
CHEPSTOW
NEWPORT

The Borderland of England and Wales

Preface

Every frontier, every critical line where two separate cultures, two systems of law, two social organizations, both meet and separate presents a heightened tension, intensified colours, a sense of drama the settled hinterlands do not know. By the nature of frontiers, they are often foothill country, even mountain country, which gives them variety, beauty and awe to begin with, and their inevitable depth and passion of history lifts the imagination into high drama, in the most profound places into tragedy.

We two who have compiled this book came to the love of the Marches by different approaches. I was born and bred in a border shire, and into a family which tended to find the westward view far more interesting than the outlook to the east, where Shropshire melds gradually into the industrial Midlands. Whenever time offered, we went west. Ruins of castles, the lovely reminders of past grief and triumph, in grey stones and green valleys, the broken beauties of churches and abbeys, all appealed strongly to my sense of history. By this time my affection for the Marches is more cerebral than simply admiration of their romantic beauty. Every landscape, every green meadow that was once a battlefield, every boundary stone where Welsh and English settled their grievances and patched up their quarrels, every lone arch left of a lost church, or rock chamber that was once covered by a long barrow, talk to me of things that happened there long ago.

Roy, on the other hand, came with an open mind, and, better still, open eyes, from the levels and enormous skies of East Anglia into this quite unfamiliar country, and saw it fresh and new, a different vision. That vision is offered here, sometimes a revelation to me, who thought I knew my borderland thoroughly. To see its felicities and secrets through other, more critical and more astonished eyes makes all the colours brighter, all the memories more poignant, and draws all the people of the past, after the battles are over, closer to reconcilation.

The Mortimers and the Crown

Ralph Mortimer, established in the central March by the Conqueror, about 1075

Roger, first cousin to Llewelyn ap Griffith through his mother, (d. 1282)

Edmund (d. 1304)   Roger

(the brothers who testified for Llewelyn after his death)

Roger, Ist Earl of March, lover of Edward II's Queen Isabella, and responsible for the king's murder (d. 1330)

Edmund (d. 1330)

Roger, restored as Earl of March by King Edward III (d. 1360)

Edmund, a child at his father's death, a royal ward, and married Philippa, daughter of the Duke of Clarence, Edward III's second son (d. 1381)

Roger, Earl of March, named by Richard II as his successor, and accepted as such (d. 1398)   Edmund, Shakespeare's Edmund Mortimer   Elizabeth, married to Henry Percy (Hotspur)

Edmund, Earl of March (d. 1425 childless)   Roger   Anne, married Richard, Earl of Cambridge, son of Edward III's fourth son, but herself descended from the second through her grandmother, Philippa

Richard of York

Edward, Earl of March, later Edward IV

Introduction

Ever since the emergence of man upon the earth, tribe has succeeded tribe by a constant incursion of the stronger into the territory of the weaker. Generations increasingly confident, with
improved equipment, increased knowledge, more sophisticated
social organization and better thought out techniques of warfare,
feeling themselves in need of more living space, and more fertile
land for tillage, have used their energies to go and look for them,
and their advanced abilities to take them. A constant swirl of
dynastic movement about the world marked the process, the
inheritors settling in the lowlands where living was easy, the
cramped resistance being pushed into the stony uplands. With the
increasing realization of differences in race and culture, the self-
confident incomers developed a taste for conquest that went
beyond the simple desire for land for its own sake, and became an
appetite for power and dominion.

In Britain, consisting as it did of offshore islands west of Europe,
with nothing known beyond but ocean, all of these aggressive
waves of invasion came from the east, from the land mass of the
continent. An early Iberian race of hunter-settlers, two distinct
waves of Celtic peoples, all preceded the coming of the Romans,
and each in turn dispossessed, to some extent, the previous incum-
bents, and drove them gradually westward into less hospitable hill
country. The Romans, though just as desirous of monopolizing the
best and most comfortable lands as their predecessors, thought
even more in terms of empire and domination, and exploitation of
natural resources such as silver and lead, and lived apart as rulers,
so that though they did influence some part of the native population into adopting their tastes and customs, they faded out with
little to show for their coming once Rome itself shrank, and called
them away to stave off its own disintegration.

The waves of inheritors continued, veering now to emerge from
the northern lands of the continent: Jutes, Angles, Saxons and
Danes. Not all were settlers, some came simply as temporary

OVERLEAF

This hill near Knighton is the site of
one of Caradoc's (Caractacus') hill-
forts.

raiders, but others came to annex and farm good land, and, as always, thrust the old inhabitants westward before them into the hills. The Brythons recoiled into the beautiful but ungentle mountains of Wales, and developed ways of living there that endured for centuries.

So the Welsh Marches had been the Welsh Marches long before the most formidable invaders of all came, to formulate and crystallize the term and the symbol: the belt of lands between the old and the new, the mountains and the plain, the white land and the black land. Of course there was intermarriage across the border; there always is across all borders, and it is in the nature of things that the wall that keeps out nine men will simply be a challenge to the tenth to climb it. But, by and large, the March of Wales existed to keep two peoples from each other's throat. Not by agreement, for the stronger of the two imposed it, and was also the power eternally ready to push it a few miles further west if the opportunity offered.

The Normans came at a late stage, when politics, privilege, and a degree of shared culture and experience with the current population of England had given them, or so they held, rights in the English crown and lands; and they came with intelligence enough, once they had established themselves, to adapt to the customs of the country they desired to settle and possess permanently, rather than simply to destroy customs wholesale and impose their own.

Shared culture and experience with the English, yes, but not with the Welsh. The whole structure of Welsh living was entirely different, tribal instead of feudal, based strongly upon kinship, in which every acknowledged son, in or out of wedlock, had his secure place and his inalienable rights. It was a system scrupulously fair, and endlessly destructive. No sooner had one strong prince established an ordered rule over a viable realm than his many sons tore the land and one another to pieces over the inheritance. Primogeniture, which at least afforded a reasonable chance of continuity, meant nothing to the Welsh. Hence their truly great administrators, like the succession of Owain Gwynedd, Llewelyn the Great and Llewelyn ap Griffith, tended to occur in alternate generations, and the status quo was never to be relied on beyond one man's lifetime.

Well before the advent of the Normans, the March of Wales,

Beneath these fields is buried the Roman town of Uriconium (Wroxeter). Some foundations and one stone wall remain in the small museum on site.

besides being a legal and also a defensive buffer zone between hostile races, had become for a long period a boundary between two kinds of Christianity. At the Synod of Whitby, in 664, the Roman rite had prevailed over the Celtic, and gradually the various regions of Celtic Christianity had given in and adopted the Roman Easter and all the other disputed points. Wales was the last to succumb. It held out until 768, and even long after that the ordinary people, untroubled by such distant decrees from overseas, clung to the old communion of the Celtic saints.

The Romans had left plenty of their traces in Wales, in the many place-names incorporating the word 'Caer', and the considerable network of their roads. This western part of the British province was heavily garrisoned, like all such remote and half-tamed regions, while the east and south-east of England was a pacified land of villas and townships, with no need of more military force than a little casual policing. There were occasional serious outbreaks, but they were rare. Wales, on the other hand, was heavily occupied because it was far from subdued. The Roman fortresses maintained themselves by constant vigilance in a hostile country. At the northern end of the March, Chester and its attendant forts kept a strong hold; in the south, at Caerwent, Usk and Caerleon the grip was equally strong. But in the centre of the March, pacification seems to have made more progress, and Uriconium, the modern Wroxeter, from the seat of a legion blossomed into an extensive and prosperous town, mainly native in population, but wholly Roman in character.

No such Romano-British town has been found in upland Wales proper, and no peaceful villa to show that the country was safe for easy patrician living. The evidence is that the Welsh, if suppressed by force, were never tamed. They kept their Celtic language and their ancient customs long after the Romans were gone back to their collapsing empire and their threatened capital city.

In later years the Welsh of the northern March came up against a formidable enemy in the alien and pagan kingdom of Northumbria, and for a time success went back and forth impartially between the two. About the year 615 King Aethelfrith of Northumbria won a victory over the Welsh near Chester, killing their chieftain. Then the Welshman Cadwallon fought a long and eventually successful campaign against Edwin of Northumbria, but his triumph was shortlived. Edwin rallied his forces again to invade Wales, and for a time Cadwallon was forced to retire to Ireland; but he returned to make common cause with King Penda of Mercia, and between them they turned the tables on Northumbria to such a tune that Edwin was killed, and his lands methodically ravaged with a view to ruining their power to maintain an effective threat in the future. This was the point at which a notable figure appeared. A younger son of Aethelfrith and a devoted convert to Christianity, Oswald rallied the English of Northumbria to a great battle with the Welsh at Heavenfield, close to the Roman wall, and won a great victory, in which Cadwallon died.

It was not the Welsh, but Penda of Mercia, who brought about at last the death of Oswald, at the battle of Maserfield, for the location of which the evidence points to Oswestry, named for the dead king and saint. All this long contention began with the Christian Welsh fending off these northerners of Teutonic origin and pagan religion, and ended with the creation of an English saint and martyr from among the ranks of the invaders.

It was by no means an unknown thing for alliances to form across the barrier, as in the case of Cadwallon and Penda, for mutual benefit but for very different motives. Cadwallon was simply carrying on with his quasi-crusade against a heathen threat, even though by the end of the feud Northumbria had substantially converted to Christianity. Penda came willingly into the alliance to curb the growing power of the northern kingdom, since it was his own ambition to achieve the supremacy over the whole country, and Northumbria was threatening to get there first. Such alliances were usually brief, but not infrequent. Necessity sometimes brought together some very strange bedfellows.

A later king of Mercia, Offa, marked out the boundary visibly, late in the eighth century, by constructing the dyke that bears his name. It was a tremendous undertaking, and must have employed armies of labourers to dig out the ditch and pile the earth rampart literally from sea to sea. That is how the records describe it,

King Offa of Mercia built a dyke to separate England from Wales in the eighth century. The dyke runs for 80 miles from the Dee estuary in the north to Chepstow on the Severn estuary in the south.

though parts of its course at either end are difficult to trace after so many centuries. Offa was neighbour to Wales throughout the length of it, his holding then being so extensive, and clearly the dyke was meant as a partial defence against the Welsh, for throughout its course the ditch is kept to the westward side, and where a convenient escarpment offered with its steep to westward, the dyke followed it. But it was as much a legal as a defensive boundary, and its very creation signified that Mercia had no intention of striking beyond in search of conquest, just as surely as it stated Mercia's intention of resisting any encroachment from the western side. The man who crossed it in either direction knew under which law he stood, and had better behave accordingly.

The line the dyke takes shows that at the time of its construction some areas of accessible lowland at either end, now accepted as Welsh, were then held by England. Even such borders can be fluid, as either side has the temporary ascendancy. But since Offa placed the boundary where he did, it was plain that he had no intention of pushing it further west. So far as the now established English were concerned, they were content to hold what they held, and let Wales alone.

At the time of the Norman invasion England, under Edward the Confessor, himself half-Norman in blood and wholly Norman in upbringing and sympathies, had for some years become accustomed to the king's tastes and ideas, and he had encouraged some of his Norman kin and friends to settle in the country. There was already a strong Norman colonization in Herefordshire. Duke William's coming caused no great upheaval in customs and ways of living, which made things much easier for him in England than if he had brought in a completely alien regime. But in Wales there was not only a strong national feeling, but a self-confident ascendancy along the border, with a number of formerly English enclaves in Welsh hands.

It was natural that William should base his first moves on the support he could be certain of in Hereford. He made his cousin William FitzOsbern Earl of Hereford, and gave him a free hand in that part of the March. But further north the Welsh brothers Bleddyn and Rhiwallon joined forces with the great Mercian nobleman Edric the Wild, and a little later also with the two brother earls Edwin of Mercia and Morcar of Northumbria, in the first serious revolt against the new regime. The resistance of the earls did not last long, but Edric and the Welsh held out for some years, Edric being the last to make his peace with the king, in 1070. From then on Wales was left without allies, to take care of its own cause alone.

William FitzOsbern, Earl of Hereford, was the first of the successful Marcher earls, and one of the most intelligent, as well as the most energetic. He made himself master of all Gwent, but having established his supremacy had the good sense to behave with consideration towards the tenants of the lands he had subdued, leaving their holdings in their hands, and coming to amicable terms with the Welsh prince of the region by granting him certain manors in English land, to fend off in advance any future raiding from that quarter.

His successor was fool enough to enter into a conspiracy against King William, which put the earl in prison for life, abolished the earldom for the foreseeable future, and halted what might otherwise have been the early conquest of the south of Wales.

In the north William installed Hugh d'Avranches, one of his ablest supporters, as Earl of Chester, with one Robert of Rhuddlan as his chief lieutenant, and Robert, ambitious to achieve the same high status for himself, built castles at Rhuddlan and Degannwy as safe bases for further penetration into Wales.

In the central March, William's kinsman Roger de Montgomery became Earl of Shrewsbury, and forthwith built castles at his town of Shrewsbury and at Montgomery, where he named his fortress and the borough below after his original property in France. Among his tenants and henchmen were Ralph Mortimer, the Corbets of Caus, and Rainald the Sheriff, who carved out the holding of Maesbury and Oswestry.

All these Marcher earldoms were virtually palatines, held by their lords as independently as the country was held by the king. They were placed where they were for the purpose of keeping the border securely without having to refer matters to the Crown, and to push onward into Welsh lands as personal conquerors whenever and wherever they could. They constituted a third estate, very different from the shire concept which governed the body of the kingdom. They were a powerful weapon of the Crown, but at times an extremely dangerous threat to it. Kings gambled on the accuracy of their judgement of men before they granted these unprecedented privileges in exchange for immense responsibilities; and sometimes they lost their stakes.

With the Welsh chiefs of the north either prisoners or defeated, by the year 1094 the conquest of Gwynedd seemed to be almost complete, through the encroachments from Chester and Shrewsbury. It was an illusory supremacy. The Welsh were by no means finished yet, and the apparent domination was no more real than that achieved earlier by the Romans; an untamed native population was held in check only by a series of well-garrisoned castles, from which the Norman lords emerged only in such force as to guarantee their survival. But in a tribal society where loyalty was due only to a regional dynasty, not a national idea, there were bound to be Welsh princes who for their own interests made common cause occasionally with the intruders, even against rivals of their own race. The idea of a Welsh nation was still to come.

Before the death of Henry I in 1135, the Norman rule seemed very firmly established over the whole of Wales, at least as this rule by alien force. Even in the realm of the Church, penetration was deep, for three of the bishoprics of the country had been brought to acknowledge the supremacy of the diocese of Canterbury, even though only one of the three newly installed bishops, Bernard of St David's, was actually a Norman. The fourth Welsh diocese, St Asaph's, was left in abeyance for many years, being situated in land so largely influenced by England but surrounded by Welsh territory that it presented somewhat of a problem to manage.

More hurtful still, the Normans, confronted with parish churches in their new property dedicated to Celtic saints of whom they had never heard, took to eradicating Teilo, Cynidr and Teulyddog in favour of Peter, Paul, Thomas and Nicholas, saints internationally known and approved. Even St David himself lost one of his most revered shrines to St Andrew, though later it dawned upon the Normans that it would be wise to defer to his prestige in the country. The old Celtic form of the *clas*, the

RIGHT

Henry III built Montgomery Castle early in the thirteenth century to safeguard the route into Wales, a route which followed an old Roman road.

college of canons, was also misunderstood and disapproved, and either disbanded or replaced by a more rigid monastic foundation.

The death of Henry I removed the strong personality and firm hand which had brought about the apparent triumph of the new men, but even before that some other strong personalities had been busy quietly enlarging the power and extent of Gwynedd. The sons of the old prince Griffith ap Cynan, notably Owain, had made good use of the time while the Normans were concentrating on the south of the country, and as soon as Henry died, blazing revolt broke out everywhere. Gower, Gwent and Cardigan fell back into Welsh hands, and in the middle March the castles of Caus and Bromfield near Wrexham were captured, along with parts of Maelienydd, and more to the south Llandovery, Usk and Caerleon. King Stephen, who had made haste to take possession of the English throne and been crowned late in 1135, tried ineffectively to combat the encroachments, but very soon had his hands full at home, when the Empress Maud, Henry's last remaining legitimate child, landed in England to make her own bid for sovereignty as the legal heiress, and the long years of civil war began.

It so happened that almost all the magnates of the March took the side of the empress, so that the solid wall of their personal armies completely blocked the way into Wales against any campaign the king might mount against the rebels. At the same time this situation made it impossible for the Marcher lords to make any attempt at reconquering their lost territories to westward; they were fully occupied at home, and could do no more than hold on to what they still possessed.

The Welsh made hay while the sun shone. By the end of the English anarchy, when Henry II became king, Owain Gwynedd had added most of central Wales to his northern princedom, and rolled back the March almost to Chester. The tide was reversed; Norman barons now held on tightly to limited and isolated enclaves within a land confidently and aggressively Welsh. Nor was the new king, however competent and determined, able to give any attention to the matter of Wales for the first few years of his reign, having more than enough to do in restoring order in England, demolishing all the unlicensed castles opportunist outlaws had built during

Chester Abbey was founded in 1092 and in 1542 the abbey church became the cathedral. Most of the existing fabric is the result of rebuilding which was carried out from 1280 to 1460. The re-facing of the sandstone walls was carried out in the nineteenth century.

the chaos, and calling it to the attention of over-ambitious lordlings that they now had a very different overlord to deal with. Even when he could dust his hands after that clean-up, he had to give some attention to his holdings in Normandy and Anjou. Wales was a minor concern, but not forgotten.

Henry's first inexperienced but determined attempt to curb the activities of Owain, though at one point it almost cost the king his life, also effectively showed his opponent not only the formidable mettle of the king himself, but also the immense forces he was capable of putting into the field. Owain, always a realist, wisely came to terms, which cost him the most easterly of his gains but otherwise did not greatly penalize him. In a later crisis, when both Owain in the north and Rhys ap Griffith in the south were in arms together, Henry staged the most enormous and resolute attack ever so far launched against Wales, and saw it come to utter disaster over the Welsh mountains in furious storms and gales, which bogged down his huge host and ruined half his commissariat, so that he was forced to retreat ignominiously into England and abandon the campaign, leaving Owain and his allies in possession of all they had won. To which, shortly, Owain added Rhuddlan, and the fort the English had built at Basingwerk.

But Henry, too, was a realist. He reviewed the Welsh problem in the context of all the other responsibilities that waited on his attention, and gave up all thought of setting out to conquer Wales.

At his death in 1170 Owain Gwynedd was securely in possession of all his northern lands, and acknowledged as pre-eminent among all the princes of Wales.

A period of sensible truce and tolerance set in for the following years, during which England made no serious attempt to take over Wales, and Wales entered into civilized diplomatic relations with England. Doubtless there were local brushes across the border sometimes, and certainly there were the usual fratricidal squabbles between too many brothers contending for too little land among the Welsh princedoms; as, for instance, in Gwynedd, where Owain's achievement was rapidly dismembered by his sons by two marriages, plus at least one (one of the best and the first to die), the poet-warrior Hywel, who was born out of wedlock. But basically there was cautious truce, while Norman-Welsh marriages were made, and English manors bestowed on Welsh allies. If Henry II had not had much success in managing Wales by brute force, he made a much better job of it by diplomacy. Unfortunately the phase ended with Henry's death and the accession of Richard who, obsessed with distant Crusades and the money to finance them, was not at all disposed to tackle the laborious, essential business of being a sensible king of England.

Richard I spent very little of the ten years or so of his reign in England, and had no interest in it apart from extracting from it as much money as possible for his overseas adventures. He troubled Wales hardly at all, leaving two strong personalities to contend there for dominance, Owain Gwynedd's grandson Llewelyn ab Iorwerth, and Gwenwynwyn of Powys. But when John succeeded his brother in 1199, armed with some experience as a Marcher baron himself, he set to work to control the country by intervening in this rivalry only with a view to maintaining the balance of power beween them, by judiciously applying his favour or disfavour according to circumstances, and thus keep them busy trying to outdo each other, without any time or energy to cause trouble for the Crown. At a time when the king was finding it convenient to favour Llewelyn he conferred upon him an ally more valuable than any minor prince by giving him his own natural daughter Joan in marriage. Joan had been brought up at the court of her grandmother, Eleanor of Aquitaine, and was cultured, able, gifted and highly intelligent, and the partnership lasted gloriously for life, in spite of one tragic love affair on Joan's part, and a single year of estrangement. She was always her husband's best ambassador and strongest support. The duel with King John, conducted sometimes in arms, sometimes by diplomatic means, went on for many years with fluctuating fortunes, until the many external troubles which the king brought on himself, both in Church matters and in relations with his own barons, gave Llewelyn the dominance, which he carried unrelentingly until John's death in 1216, and beyond into the reign of the boy heir, Henry III. From then until his own death in 1240 the prince of Gwynedd had no rival. He had earned his title of 'the Great', and was respected and dealt with on equal terms by the English authorities.

Intermarriage between notabilities from either side of the border had by this time greatly complicated but also tended to stabilize English–Welsh relations. The marriage contracts of Llewelyn's children illustrate the development. By Joan he had only one son, who married an heiress of the de Breose family, but four daughters, all of whom married Marcher lords, two of them making two such marriages. Gwenllian married William de Lacy; Helen married John, Earl of Chester; Gwladus married first, Reginald de Breose, and second, Ralph Mortimer; and Margaret, after the death of her first husband John de Breose, married Walter Clifford. Every one a baron of the March.

There was also one illegitimate son, Griffith, to precipitate the

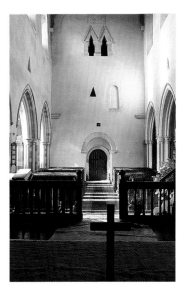

At Deerhurst, near to Kempsey and also on the banks of the River Severn, is one of the finest Saxon churches in England. This picture of the tenth-century west wall was taken from the eighth-century nave. The nave arches are Early English and result from re-modelling in the twelfth century.

OVERLEAF

In these fields beside the River Lugg at Pilleth Edmund Mortimer and Owen Glendower fought on a summer day in 1401.

usual disastrous clash between English and Welsh law when the great prince died. For by English law only David, Joan's son, had any claim to inherit, whereas by Welsh law every acknowledged son had an equal claim on his father's property. It was the Welsh tradition, and the bards in particular upheld it, and condemned any infringement. But long contact with his far more powerful neighbour had shown Llewelyn that only the succession of David, legitimate by any standards and grandson to the king of England, of irreproachable pedigree, could be acceptable without question to the English, and ensure the continuance of progress towards a Welsh nation, entrenched and recognized. The only way for a much poorer and weaker state to resist being swallowed by feudal England was to borrow some, at least, of the strengths of feudalism itself. Llewelyn, before he died, named David as his sole heir.

Griffith, the elder and illegitimate son, was rash and turbulent by temperament, and had already in the past given his father trouble and been imprisoned for a time. David took the precaution of keeping him prisoner after his father's death, until the relationship with England should be clarified, and incarcerated Griffith's eldest son, Owain, with him, anticipating trouble. Griffith's wife promptly removed herself and her younger children secretly, and fled to Shrewsbury to place them and her husband's cause in the hands of King Henry. But the second son, Llewelyn, then about twelve years old, remained in Gwynedd, and within the year he was known to be in arms and fighting for his Uncle David and for the Welsh cause. King Henry had acknowledged David as Prince of Gwynedd, but had no intention of leaving him in possession of any of the other territories Llewelyn the Great had added to his princedom. By encouraging dispossessed lords to take to the law, and eventually by launching an attack against North Wales, Henry set out to reduce the country to its old state of subjugation. Naturally the two prisoners, Griffith and Owain, were handy tools once he got possession of them, and so far from being freed, father and son found themselves only exchanging David's prison for close confinement in the Tower of London. Henry now held all the family, except for Llewelyn, now approaching fourteen, the age of manhood in Wales, and already proven a man, for he had distinguished himself in the defence of Gwynedd, his uncle's attempt at holding a nation together, and his grandfather's vision of what that nation could become.

One of the king's tools slipped through his fingers when Griffith, attempting escape from his high prison in the Tower, fell and was killed. Owain remained the next candidate for a very limited and subservient inheritance, if David could be suppressed; and Owain willingly promised, if he should ever be installed, to hold his princedom from King Henry, like any ordinary baron, and to be subject to England once and for all. He was sent to Chester to rally the traditionalists who supported his right, but when he heard that David had died of illness in Aber, he broke away from his guards and made off in haste to claim his right as the elder son.

On the advice of the council, the two brothers Owain and Llewelyn agreed to share the rule in Gwynedd, while dividing the lands fairly between them, and making suitable provision for the two younger brothers. This state continued only a few years, for Owain nursed his dissatisfaction at being only co-ruler of a greatly reduced land, the necessary peace with England having forced the surrender of many of Llewelyn the Great's conquests. He joined secretly with his youngest brother, David, to launch an attack against Llewelyn, and was decisively defeated, deposed, and imprisoned. Henceforth Llewelyn was Gwynedd, in one person. The story of his enormous achievement thereafter, complicated by the divided loyalties of young David, brought up from five-years-old to his late teens in the English court, and torn every way by conflicting affections, provides the climax to the history of independent Wales.

It also poses two huge personalities in head-on collision; for the young Prince Edward had been made Earl of Chester and endowed with all the Middle Country, the four cantrefs east of the Conwy, and was shortly to become, even during his father's lifetime, the real power in England. Henry III had come to the throne as a charming child of nine, and virtually remained a charming child all his life, or at best an unstable adolescent. He had considerable graces and virtues, but he had also the weaknesses of immaturity, in particular an inability to maintain balance and moderation. His tantrums were anything but charming. He could never be in the wrong, it was always someone else's fault, and if he was made to look foolish, or humiliated in any way, someone would be made to pay for it savagely thereafter. His long and vicious persecution of Hubert de Burgh is a case in point. So is the violence with which he turned on his favourite Angevin ministers when it came out that they had embroiled him in suspicion of involvement in the murder of the Earl Marshall in Ireland. He was forever nestled in your bosom or had a knife in your back. In the field he was no very formidable opponent, and no match for the valour and generalship of Llewelyn.

But his son and heir, with the same long memory for injuries and even more vindictiveness in avenging them, had also the ability to learn, and a chill control over his passions which made him far more daunting, plus a relentless efficiency in arms, both personally and in commanding others. Given the resources he could field, far beyond anything Wales could muster in numbers and equipment, he was a match for any prince living.

But Edward was not yet king. Llewelyn began the recovery of his grandfather's gains with all the bitter complaints of oppressed Welshmen in the Middle Country and elsewhere ringing in his ears and urging him on. The four cantrefs fell to him, the boundary pushed right back within sight of Chester, where the hated seat of English administration was based. Castles fell before him, or were surrounded and left isolated and useless while the tide of conquest flowed past them. Meirionydd, Cardigan, Gwerthrynion snatched from the Mortimers – all were added to the recovered lands of Wales.

It was the period when King Henry's own barons were beginning to make common cause against his feckless proceedings, and to demand reforms, and there was neither money nor inclination to take up arms for him against the Welsh. The Welshry of other regions caught the contagion, and rose to get rid of their overlords. The king did make one ineffective sally from Chester, but it was his last venture in person against Wales, and ended in retreat. Early in 1258 Llewelyn was strong enough to call together all but one of the princes at a great council, where he received their homage and assumed the title of Prince of Wales. The absentee, ominously, was Griffith ap Gwenwynwyn of Powys, always his chief rival and enemy, already almost more English than the English, and prepared to take their side for his own interests against the assembly of Wales.

This ford near Montgomery on the River Severn is where the Welsh and English often met to discuss their differences.

By conquest where opportunity offered, and intelligent use of truce agreements when he could get them, Llewelyn guarded and preserved his gains through the period of the Barons' War, which brought him and his newly moulded country into alliance for a time with the reform movement led by Simon de Montfort, the Earl of Leicester. It was at a time when Simon's cause was at its most desperate, before his death at the battle of Evesham, that he made an agreement, in the name of the king who was then virtually his prisoner, granting to Llewelyn all his conquests and recognition of his title as Prince of Wales, and also betrothed to Llewelyn his only daughter, Eleanor. Three months later the champion of the reform was dead, the king freed, and Edward the real power in England. But there was a long and debilitating struggle before all the last fires of revolt were quenched, and Llewelyn was able to exact from the king confirmation of all that had been promised him by Simon.

On 29 September 1267, at the ford of Rhyd Chwima by Montgomery, Llewelyn and King Henry met formally, and Llewelyn did homage for lands and titles which granted him in full everything he had fought for, including the homage of all the lesser Welsh princes. The Peace of Montgomery was his triumph.

During the rest of King Henry's life relations between England and Wales remained peaceful, even cordial. An annual payment due for the acknowledgement of his royal right was regularly paid by Llewelyn, and all exchanges were correct and amicable, though in some places the Marcher lords ventured some infringements of the terms of peace, such as beginning the building of castles against the terms agreed, or encroaching across borders. But nationally all went well, and complaints on either side were duly dealt with, with reasonable fairness.

But after the king's death, when Edward returned from his Crusade to be crowned, things deteriorated rapidly. The rot had set in even before the new king landed, for his proxies in his absence had begun to behave with an arrogance Llewelyn resented, and had aroused his suspicions that moves were being plotted against him. Edward, on the other hand, still nursed his bitter hatred against all the de Montfort family, and interpreted any contact with a member of that clan, even Eleanor, as threatening a new baronial upheaval. In view of the total defeat of the former alliance, his fear seems irrational, but hatred is never rational. Llewelyn's wariness in dealing with a new man seems merely sound sense. But whatever the causes, justified or unjustified, the two began to distrust each other.

In view of all that happened afterwards, I think that once Edward was in power, conquest was inevitable, no matter what Llewelyn might have done. Close neighbour to a smaller and more vulnerable land, Edward's nature could not stop short of grasping at every yard of it. He proved as much by attempting the same later, and with even more furious greed and hatred, against

RIGHT

High in the Brecon Beacons, in a minor wilderness, rises Nant Ddu – the Black Brook.

This is now the entrance to Abbey Dore; before the nave was demolished (to the right of picture) it was the crossing. The gallery for the minstrels and choir now stands against the blocked-up west arch.

Scotland. Scotland, besides being lucky in the paladins who rose in her defence, was luckier still in her geography. No massive supply line, such as an army in the field demands, could ever have been maintained into the north of Scotland, all that immense journey beset everywhere with admirable locations for ambush. By comparison a man could ride across Wales in a day, and even the heights of Snowdonia could finally be encircled like a castle under siege.

So the mutual distrust burned into battle in the end. Edward spent much of 1276 preparing the way by giving a free hand to the Marcher assemblies gathered in three groups, at Chester, Montgomery and Carmarthen (still a royal enclave). All three moved into action locally, eating away the border regions commote by commote: from Chester northern Powys was occupied, from Montgomery southern Powys, from Carmarthen much of Cardigan. When the groundwork was done, Edward himself with the feudal host and his mercenaries, which he was beginning to prefer, moved in along the north coast, securing Flint and Rhuddlan, and building forts there, later to become stone castles. He brought up a fleet from the Cinque Ports to possess Anglesey and reap or burn the corn harvest. Llewelyn recognized reality and sought terms. At Aberconwy he accepted terms of peace which deprived him of all his lands except the hereditary princedom of Gwynedd west of Conwy. He kept his title of Prince of Wales, and was free to bring suit at law over lands to which he claimed rights as against other magnates, such as Griffith ap Gwenwynwyn, who by this time was adapting his style and title into English by calling himself de la Pole, from his castle of Pool, and behaving entirely as an English baron. But Llewelyn's experience of Edward's manipulation of law was frustrating in the extreme, since only Edward was allowed to interpret it.

However, for four years Llewelyn accepted his reduced status with dignity, and kept all the terms of the settlement. At least it had at last united him with Eleanor de Montfort. Edward permitted the marriage to take place, and even presided over the celebrations.

This courtship and marriage of Llewelyn and Eleanor seems to me a most remarkable story, and suggests a genuine and resolute love, even though for about thirteen years it was the very picture of an *amour de loin*, such as Geoffrey Rudel and Bernard of Ventadorn sang about. As far as I can discover, the two had never met until Edward somewhat grudgingly brought them together for one meeting before the marriage. Eleanor was a child when her father promised her to the Prince of Wales. At that time Llewelyn was at the height of his power and achievement, with a new nation to sustain, and had every possible incentive to marry and produce heirs to follow him. His betrothed had been removed to France by her mother, Edward's aunt, who had promised Edward never to make any move in renewal of the de Montfort influence, and therefore would not countenance the marriage. Almost certainly his council must have urged the prince to take a noble Welsh wife and bring a son into the picture to ensure the succession. He did no such thing. He waited doggedly until he could have Eleanor. He was turned fifty when at last they married. More remarkable still, Eleanor in France, a most desirable match and probably courted by numbers of eligible young noblemen, also waited. It is likely that her mother would have been very happy to match her and see her secure in life; certainly she can have given her daughter no encouragement in holding out for so perilous a husband. But Eleanor waited, as Llewelyn waited, and in the end they had their way. It was no ordinary medieval marriage that was finally celebrated at the door of Worcester cathedral.

Since so much of Wales had recoiled into English control, all the inhabitants soon had their old grievances back in full. The behaviour of the king's officials throughout the Middle Country was high-handed and arrogant in the extreme, tax extortions were bitterly resented, and any suits at law which affected Welsh interests invariably ended in favour of the other party. It was not Llewelyn who began the last confrontation in arms, but David, himself suffering under the regime, and acting as a channel for the seething indignation of all his fellow countrymen, driven to despair. He rose in well-organized revolt, the entire Middle Country with him, seized the castle of Hawarden, isolated Rhuddlan and gave the signal for the south to rise as effectively against the royal castles of Aberystwyth, Llandovery and Carreg Cennen.

Confronted with a situation in which he had to choose, not between Wales and neutrality, for that was impossible, but between Wales and taking up arms for England against Wales, Llewelyn in fact had no choice at all. It was inconceivable that he should ever respond to a call from Edward to fight against his own people. He did what he had to do, raised all his own forces and joined his brother.

This time Edward was determined to make an end. Up to this last enormously costly campaign, the conquest of Wales had been achieved not by the Crown, but by individual Marcher lords on their own initiative and for their own enlargement. Now Edward raised the greatest force in men and ships, in feudal dues and paid mercenaries that had ever been used against Wales. Advancing as usual along the north coast from Chester, he launched before him hordes of woodcutters and labourers to fell the forests and open wide roads ahead, and posted companies of archers to protect them while they worked. And where previously he had followed the old practice of a summer campaign, a quick in-and-out before winter closed in, this time he made such formidable provision in

food supplies, masons for castle-building, and clearance of woodland, that it was plain he was aiming at a permanent stay and a war
pursued to the end. Gradually Llewelyn and David were forced
into the mountains of Snowdonia, beyond Conwy. Anglesey was
again occupied from the sea, and the harvest lost. There were successes, too, but the end was inevitable. Edward had discovered that
the mountain fastnesses could indeed be encircled and starved into
submission.

John Peckham, Archbishop of Canterbury, well meaning but
totally without understanding of the Welsh, and insensitive to their
feelings, made an attempt to bring about peace, and brought back
proudly and complacently to the princes terms grudgingly prised
out of Edward, terms which were not merely unacceptable but to
Welshmen insulting. Llewelyn might have submitted and been
established in some part of England as a baron worth a thousand
pounds a year, with his title to the baronage heritable, if he had

Llangua church stands off the main
Hereford–Abergavenny road near
Pontrillas. It was founded by the
Abbey of Lyre in Calvados soon after
the Norman Conquest.

been willing to cede to this crass king the barren wilds of Snowdonia. Edward probably never understood that in making an offer he thought generous he had made himself contemptible. With dignity, without even passion – for the case was gone beyond that – Llewelyn refused. The war continued.

In the midst of the fighting Eleanor de Montfort, Princess of Wales, had died at Aber in giving birth to a daughter, Gwenllian, whose story is one of lifelong imprisonment, almost from birth. Like all the spoils of war she fell into the hands of Edward, along with David's seven little girls and two young sons. None of these dangerous enemies was ever to be allowed to mate and breed. The girls were all distributed among the convents of the Order of Sempringham, the boys vanished into the dungeons of Bristol castle. Edward was afraid of Llewelyn's clan, even in their cradles.

However, he never succeeded in parading Llewelyn in chains at his triumph, for the prince died in an obscure skirmish in the south, after a battle from which, according to tradition, he was lured away to some secret meeting, never explained. He died still in arms, still not defeated. It was his brother David who was left to take up the title and the battle, and to pay the kind of price eventually that the Edwards of this world demand.

This time the whole of Wales was subjugated, pinned down by a rash of tremendous castles in stone, built to be permanent and impregnable, and garrisoned in strength. But the Marcher baronies with their privileges and duties continued to be formidable weapons in the English strategy, and in the feuding alliances that came later. In the year 1300 the resounding names still echoed down the March: Lacy of Denbigh, Grey of Ruthin, Warenne of Bromfield, FitzAlan of Oswestry and Clun, Mortimer of Chirk, Maelienydd and Radnor, Bohun of Brecon, de Breose of Gower, Clare of Glamorgan. They all retained their palatine lordships as distinct from land subject to the Crown.

There was to be one more upheaval between Welsh and English, where alliances crossed the border and brought together against the usurped sovereignty of Henry IV, Mortimer of the central March, the Percys of Northumberland, and Owen Glendower, champion of Wales. Percy and Mortimer were already joined by the marriage of Elizabeth Mortimer to Hotspur, and the king's refusal to ransom her brother Edmund Mortimer from his captivity in Wales resulted in Edmund marrying Glendower's daughter Catherine, and joining his father-in-law's campaign against the Crown, thus cementing the tripartite alliance which fought and lost the battle of Shrewsbury.

The Wars of the Roses, too, saw a number of battles fought along the March: at Blore Heath, at Mortimer's Cross, at Ludlow. And during this period, about 1473, the Council of the Marches was formed to administer the principality. Its main seat was at Ludlow, a circumstance which brought the young Philip Sidney to school in Shrewsbury, when his father Sir Henry was Lord President of the Council, a post he held from 1559 to 1586.

OVERLEAF

The Stiperstones at Cold Hill near Church Stretton were mined for lead by the Romans. This is now designated an area of outstanding natural beauty.

This tomb in Moreton Corbet church to Sir Robert Corbet and his wife is dated 1513.

In the Abbey Cwm Hir valley among the hills of mid-Wales Llewelyn-ap-Griffith is buried.

But the Marches were still the Marches, with their special privileges and formidable independence, and now somewhat of a thorn in the flesh of the Crown, until the Acts of Union of 1536 to 1543. These parliamentary measures 'incorporated, united and annexed' Wales to England, and made it a political unity by abolishing the Welsh Marcher lordships, and establishing throughout the country the English shire system, in thirteen counties administered by sheriffs and justices of the peace. English common law became the law of Wales, English became the language of law and administration, and officials were required to be fluent in it. Cultivated Welshmen kept their own tongue in literary and common use, but naturally there was some effect on its general use, since official posts and advancement depended on being able to speak English. But the Acts of Union did guarantee Welshmen equality with the English before the law, and ironed out a number of injustices.

The Welsh Marches as a separate force were abolished, but the belt of country that constituted the March remains, ambivalent between the mountains of the west and the softer valleys of the east, beautiful, varied and vibrant with history, a land of castles, monasteries, heroes and saints. Still as separate as ever, home to either race, alien to both. It depends which blood you have in your own veins, to which shed blood in this soil your nerves respond, here where they fought one another to the death, and have left their green, solitary graves, their rock-hewn monuments and their ruined oratories to tell the tale. The bards may have departed, and taken their harps with them, but a breeze ruffling the moist grasses of Abbey Cwm Hir can still sound like a lament, and the roll of thunder over the rock of Montgomery like a war-trumpet calling to arms. But the line of the March also held those few agreed places where Welsh and English came together to sort out their differences, hear complaints, do justice fairly, and try to restore harmony between neighbour and neighbour. Not dividing, but bringing together. Edward, Llewelyn, the Mortimers, the Clares, Lacy, FitzAlan, Bohun, all the princes are quiet enough now. The wars, we trust, are over.

Detail from the north wall of the Chapter House at Wenlock Priory showing an intersecting arch design of the twelfth century.

OVERLEAF

This is part of the fertile valley which bestrides the River Monnow between Grosmont and Skenfrith.

The Normans in Gwent

The southernmost extremes of the March, the ambivalent land of Gwent, too Welsh to be England, too English to be Wales, has always hovered elusively between the two, often claimed by both, occasionally disputed in arms by both. Here the rich soil of Herefordshire and Gloucestershire invades the starker foothills of Wales, desirable, accessible land, fertile and profitable, only made more delectable by the ridges of hills that overhang and shelter its valleys. Here the Normans made their first inroads into Wales, from the early colony encouraged in Herefordshire by Edward the Confessor, and under the very competent leadership of William FitzOsbern, first Norman Earl of Hereford. His enterprise began so soon after the Conquest that it is plain King William considered his successful invasion to have entitled him to possession of the whole island territory, and it remained only to make good the position in fact. By 1070 FitzOsbern had almost accomplished the feat in the south. His death in 1071 halted the process of expansion, since his son frittered away everything the father had achieved by a pointless conspiracy against the king, to his own ruin. However, some of the most resounding names of the great Marcher families echo to this day in Gwent: Marshall, Bigod, de Clare, Hastings, de Burgh. The remains of their massive fortresses and the lovely ruins of their monastic foundations dapple the gracious riverside meadows and the uplands of the old Roman province. For if they brought their household armies with them, they brought their piety, too, with no sense of incongruity, and built churches and convents as well as castles.

One of the many splendid monuments
in Gloucester Cathedral is this wooden
effigy of Robert, Duke of Normandy
who died in 1134.

Chepstow Castle

T he west door was suddenly flunt open, and armour gleamed in the faint red glow from the altar, outlining a big man in light mail, with two or three others looming at his shoulders.

'Would you break sanctuary yet again?' said Hubert, advancing clear of his companions.

'God forbid!' said a deep, hearty voice. 'We are not come to haul you out of your refuge, my lord, only reverently to bid you come forth with us, all three, if you want your freedom. Ride now, question after! We have horses for all, here at the door, and by the time my lads have led the sheriff's men twice round the streets of Devizes, and got clean out again, we can be some five miles west of here.'

'Dear God, is this true?' asked Hubert, trembling. 'I cannot see you well, but I should know your voice, surely. You would not torture me with hope only to hurl me back into hell, would you?'

'No, faith, it's not hell we're bound for, but Severnside. If you want my name, it's Gilbert Basset of Compton, and Richard Siward is outside with the horses. Before noon tomorrow, if you stir quickly now, we can be at the ferry at Aust, and tomorrow you shall sleep, free men the three of you, and welcome, in the Earl Marshal's castle of Chepstow.'

* * *

King Henry might rage as he would, deal out penalties and reproaches left and right, turn his sheriff of Wiltshire loose on the possessions of every man who could be implicated, declare rescued and rescuers alike outlaw — which in fact he had only very dubious right to do, they never having been convicted at law — and seize every manor they had left within his reach, but nothing provided him consolation for this humiliating defeat. De Burgh was clean gone, safe over the Severn in Chepstow, the two daring squires gone with him, and doubtless thumbing their noses from the ramparts at all the power of England.

THE MARRIAGE OF MEGGOTTA

On the west bank of the River Wye, Chepstow Castle was started within ten years of the conquest by William FitzOsbern and has been extended over many centuries.

The rescue of Hubert de Burgh from his sanctuary in Devizes, along with the two young men who had attempted the same feat earlier, and been shut in with him, took place in November 1233. In April of the following year the third Marshal Earl of Pembroke was killed in Ireland, and the constitutional conflict between his reforming party and the Crown resolved through the mediation of Archbishop Edmund Rich, thus incidentally putting an end to the persecution of Hubert de Burgh, at least for a time. Henry III's highly volatile loves and hates had been fatal to many people, none more to be deplored than Richard Marshal.

Chepstow was already a century and a half old at that time, for it was one of the earliest of the Norman castles. By 1086 the Domesday Book was reporting: 'Earl William built the castle of Estriguil'. The Welsh name, meaning 'the bend of the river', was still in use in the Earl Marshal's time, but gradually the English Chepstow replaced it. The castle was the strongest of all those that enabled William FitzOsbern, Earl of Hereford, to win possession of virtually the whole of Gwent, and his original building, almost uniquely for that time, was in stone. Little in the way of earthworks was needed; the cliffs of the Wye provided extremely strong protection on one side, and even from the softer inland flank the long, austere ridge on which the fortress was built would have been hard to storm. William's enormous rectangular keep, like an extension of the sheer river cliffs below, sat in a long, narrow bailey, its walls sheltering the garrison buildings within.

After Earl William's death, and the rebellion and dispossession of his successor, Chepstow was kept in Crown hands for some time, before being granted first to the family of Clare, and then, when a daughter was left as sole heiress, to the bridegroom the king chose for her, William Marshal, first and greatest of the Marshal earls of Pembroke, a redoubtable clan that exploded on England like a firework, and vanished almost as suddenly. William strengthened the eastern face of Chepstow with two round towers, providing a wide field for defensive fire.

At his death he left five sons, all of whom in turn succeeded to the earldom of Pembroke and died childless. William died in 1219; by 1245 the last of his sons was dead, and not one had left an heir. William the younger inherited first, and in the twelve years of his tenure added to the comforts and domestic provisions of the castle. After him came Richard, the Earl Marshal who fell into dispute with his unstable and untrustworthy king, and was killed in suspicious circumstances in 1234, after only three years. He was succeeded by Gilbert, who added to the castle its large lower bailey, with its curtain wall and strong towers. But by 1245 the last two of the Marshal brothers, Walter and Anselm, were gone after their kin, leaving the lands to be divided among their surviving sisters. Chepstow went to the eldest, Maud, and through her to her son Roger Bigod, Earl of Norfolk. Three of the greatest Marcher families, the Clares, the Marshals and the Bigods, between them had added considerably to the vast extent and strength of William FitzOsbern's original castle and town of Chepstow.

Once the Edwardian wars were over, with Wales more or less pacified, the subsequent history of the castle was comparatively uneventful, apart from a few more personal crises during the Wars of the Roses, when the unpopular Woodville kinsmen sought

This detail shows openings into the storage cellar of Chepstow Castle built in the thirteenth century. Through these openings goods could be hauled up from boats anchored below.

refuge within its walls, and were handed over to very rough justice by the garrison, who liked them no better than did their pursuers. In the Civil War the castle was held for the king, but finally came under Cromwellian cannon fire, and fell to the Puritans. It was granted to Cromwell himself, and became a barracks and a convenient prison for disapproved people. It was prison for a time to Bishop Jeremy Taylor, a High-Churchman and Royalist, and twenty-five years later, and for life, to one of the regicides, Henry Marten, who gave his name to the tower in which his rooms were situated. The whirligig of time, as usual, had brought his revenges.

Tintern Abbey

A few miles up the Wye valley from Chepstow, in green meadows by the river, with wooded hills around, lies Tintern Abbey, one of those idyllic ruins that so haunted the Romantic imagination in the late eighteenth and nineteenth centuries, and remain overwhelming even in these days, when they can no longer preserve the lovely reticence and isolation for which their sites were originally chosen. Apart from town or village, remote from the world, in solitary valleys by rivers and streams, often at the upland reaches near the source – these were the criteria for which the Cistercians looked when planning a new foundation.

This was the second such plantation in Britain, the first being at Waverley in Surrey, in 1128. Tintern was the first in Wales, founded only three years later by Walter de Clare, lord of Chepstow. Throughout the Marshal dynasty the earls of Pembroke continued to be good patrons to the young foundation. They gave lands and gifts, and the first William Marshal founded Tintern's Irish daughter house at Tintern Minor in Wexford.

The monks of Tintern gradually acquired extensive land, their chief wealth, and worked at increasing their holding by draining parts of the marshy coastal levels of Gwent, and also clearing woodland. The house became, for Wales, a comparatively wealthy one.

Roger Bigod, Earl of Norfolk, who succeeded to the lordship of Chepstow through one of the Marshal heiresses, supported the abbey with large endowments in land and gifts, and towards the

OVERLEAF

The thirteenth-century south front of Tintern Abbey which was founded by Walter FitzRichard de Clare, the Norman lord of Chepstow, in 1131.

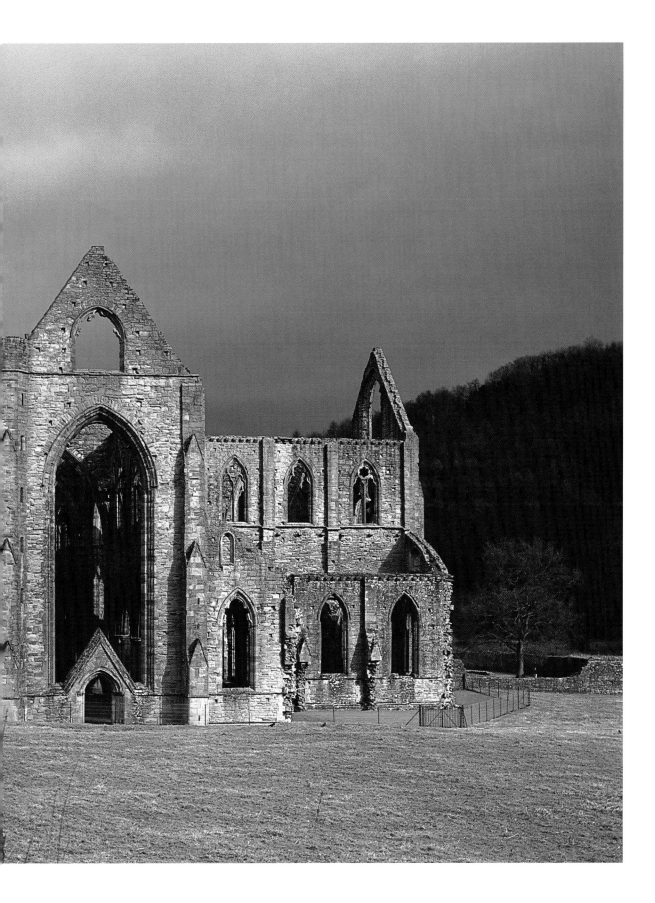

end of the thirteenth century helped the rebuilding of the church. This is the church we see today, even after the gnawings of time, the predatory attentions of Henry VIII's commissioners at the Dissolution, and the depredations of generations of enterprising local builders, still a wonder. For being founded in a solitary place, with no nearby town or large settlement, at least partially protected the stones of Tintern. They were left to be rediscovered, after the Age of Reason had ignored them as undisciplined and disorderly, by the Romantic Movement, to launch paeans of delight and awe from the poets, and keep the artists, from Turner onwards, flocking to the banks of the Wye.

Raglan Castle

Raglan castle was in the building for many years in the middle of the fifteenth century, and belongs to the extreme end of the Middle Ages, though it was erected on a motte and bailey site, which suggests there may have been a previous fortress there. It plays almost no part in the final flickerings of Welsh rebellion after the conquest, being one of the very last castles of such strength and magnificence built in the region. Its history belongs rather to the Wars of the Roses and the later Civil War, so far as military matters are concerned.

The Herbert family, who built the castle, were of the Yorkist persuasion. Indeed two of them lost their lives in the Yorkist cause. William Herbert, Earl of Pembroke, and his brother Richard were captured by the Earl of Warwick after a battle at Edgecote in 1469, and beheaded at Northampton. Another Herbert, Sir Walter, later joined Henry Tudor before he reached Shrewsbury on his march to the field of Bosworth and the Crown, bringing with him the levies of south-eastern Wales.

With the Tudor settlement, Raglan enjoyed a peaceful life, and its owners turned their energies to making it even more splendid and imposing within. In the Civil War Raglan was one of the first to declare for the king, and most of South Wales followed suit, though the Parliamentary forces captured nearby Monmouth, and provided the garrison at Raglan with some brisk local fighting. It was the last castle in the south to surrender to the victorious

A view of the gatehouse towers of Raglan Castle from the east.

Parliamentary army under Sir Thomas Fairfax, after a long siege. It was slighted, and plundered of its lead and other valuables. But it was restored to its owners by Charles II after his own Restoration.

Abergavenny Castle

Earl Roger of Hereford, son of the Miles of Gloucester who was given the Hereford title by the Empress Maud, left only daughters when he died, so the lands, but not the earldom, went in turn to each of his four brothers, all of whom died childless. One of them, Henry, was murdered by a Welsh prince, Seisyll ap Dyfnwal. The lands were then divided among Roger's daughters, and his Welsh lands, including the castle of Abergavenny, went to Bertha, who was married to one of the powerful de Breose family. Their son William de Breose inherited in 1175, and set out at once to avenge the murder of his uncle by the Welsh princeling. With the connivance of the sheriff of Herefordshire he summoned Seisyll and the other local Welsh chiefs to Abergavenny, on the pretence of informing them of an ordinance of the Crown concerning the bearing of arms. They came, unsuspecting, and were all killed within the castle. Not content with that, their murderers rode out afterwards to raid the lands and homes of their victims. Seisyll's wife was carried off prisoner, and her seven-year-old son killed in her arms.

The men of Gwent did not forget this deed of blood and treachery. Eight years later they surrounded and besieged Abergavenny castle, broke into it at dawn, took possession of all but the too-strong keep, and fired the whole castle. Then they sought out William and the sheriff, where they were engaged on building at another site, and killed the sheriff, though William managed to escape. Plenty of blood was shed along the Marches, but the massacre of Abergavenny was remembered with particular detestation.

The de Breose family were still holding Abergavenny at the time of the unhappy love affair of William de Breose, a later William, and Princess Joan, the wife of Llewelyn the Great, for that castle, along with Radnor, Hay, Huntingdon and St Clear's, was taken into Crown hands when William's death at Llewelyn's hand was known. The dead man had left only four little daughters, among whom the immense lands of his honour were divided.

OVERLEAF

The Normans built an earthwork and timber castle here about the year 1100 as yet another base for their forays into Wales. The present ruins of Abergavenny Castle date from the thirteenth century.

The Three Castles of Gwent: Grosmont, White Castle, Skenfrith

The three castles of Gwent are constantly thought of as one unit, and for all but about sixty years of their nine centuries of existence they have been in a single ownership. They lie in the valley of the Monnow and the medieval lordship of Monmouth, guarding one of the main approaches to South Wales, and like everything in medieval Gwent, they are associated with the name of William FitzOsbern, first Norman Earl of Hereford.

After the second earl's deposition for conspiracy against the Conqueror, the king was wary of leaving such a large and vital holding in one pair of hands, and bestowed the individual portions upon three separate lords; but when King Stephen assumed the crown on the death of Henry I the Welsh took the opportunity of

A view of Grosmont from the curtain wall of the castle. The spire is that of St Nicholas' church, which was begun in 1100.

rising as soon as the strong restraining hand was removed, and Stephen hastened to unite the three castles in his own hands, making restitution by granting lands elsewhere to those he displaced.

Throughout the eleventh and twelfth centuries all three castles were administered by Crown officials, well maintained as protection against Welsh raiding, and occasional serious risings, and constantly brought up-to-date in their defences. They had begun, like all the earliest castles, as earth and timber erections, and with the years they were raised to the status of powerful stone castles, such as everywhere along the March, ensuring Norman sovereignty and affording bases for further gains.

In 1201 King John granted the lordships of the three castles to Hubert de Burgh, Norfolk born, and one of the new men at whom the old nobility looked with some reservations, and even some disdain. But he was able, a good soldier, and had served the king, as later he served the young king Henry III, with absolute loyalty and efficiency. Hubert had soldiered in France, and had learned a great deal about castle-building, and in the few years of his first tenure he did some substantial building and improving at Grosmont. But while defending Chinon for the king he was taken prisoner by the French, and the lordship passed for some years into other hands. Only after John's death, when the new king was twelve years old, and Hubert his justiciar, did de Burgh recover his lordship from the de Breose family, in whose hands it then was. From 1219 to 1232 he set in hand a great programme of rebuilding at Skenfrith and Grosmont. White Castle seems to have been kept mainly as a military store and arsenal, while the other two were made more comfortably habitable, and rebuilt in the regional red sandstone.

Hubert's prosperous years came to an abrupt and startling end when he was suddenly arraigned of all manner of offences, some so far-fetched they belong only in fairy-tales, stripped of his title of Earl of Kent and all his castles and offices, and threatened with summary trial, with the implicit menace of being put to death. His fall was largely due to the unstable king's subservience to the overbearing influence of his Poitevin relatives and favourites, especially the formidable Bishop of Winchester, Peter des Roches, his nephew Peter des Rivaux, and the whole tribe of foreign hangers-

White Castle was another castle founded by the Normans, enlarged and improved in later centuries. This view is of the inner moat and chapel tower dating from the twelfth century.

on who served them. But the sheer viciousness of King Henry's hatred and persecution can only be explained by the weakness of his character, which forced him to go to extremes in order to maintain any position at all. The venom with which Hubert was hounded remains almost inexplicable.

At this time Richard, Earl Marshal, third of the line, had just come to England to take up the lordship of Pembroke and Chepstow after his elder brother's death, and he found the order of things under a king entirely subject to Poitevin influence too outrageous to be allowed to continue. He sought reform, and took up Hubert's cause; when the prisoner was rescued by other partisans of the reform party, it was at Earl Richard's castle of Chepstow that he found a safe haven.

It was the assassination of Earl Richard in Ireland that at last restored Hubert's credit in the realm, and turned Henry's venom, in terrified self-defence, against des Roches and all his creatures. The Archbishop of Canterbury, Edmund Rich, came into possession of letters which made it clear that the murder had been planned and authorized, with the royal seal to authenticate the orders, so that even if Henry himself had not been privy to the plot, it must mean that he had turned a blind eye and allowed his seal to be used by someone else without hindrance. His only defence was to turn on his closest advisers and instruments in outraged innocence, and charge them with deceiving him and abusing his trust. The position was reversed, the Poitevins banished, and the partisans of the Earl Marshal gained by his death everything they had been unable to win while he was alive. The exiles were brought home with ceremony to a meeting with the king at Gloucester, among them Hubert de Burgh. He regained his status, much of his property, and his name was regarded as cleared. He did not regain the king's favour. No one ever did who had been, even in the least degree, the cause of blackening Henry's face in public. But he was accepted, perforce. Henry waited another opportunity to exact further payment, and the castles of Gwent passed into the hands of a Crown administrator once again, until they were bestowed on the younger brother of Edward I, Edmund, Earl of Lancaster. By then, with the conquest of Wales irreversible, they were of less strategic importance. And when the dynasty of Lancaster, in the person of Henry of Bolingbroke, deposed Richard II

Skenfrith Castle is a fine example of a thirteenth-century keep, with a bailey enclosure of curtain walls between five round towers.

and assumed the crown, the castles of Gwent again became royal castles.

Barring a few convulsions of resistance during Owen Glendower's rising, they begin to pass out of history into landscape; down from mere administrative centres, through gradual decay and a number of changes of ownership, they mellowed into beautiful, haunting features of a beautiful, haunting region, and are at last in the care of the Wales they were built to resist and contain.

Gloucester

The city and earldom of Gloucester have played a prominent and often tragic part not only in Anglo-Welsh affairs, but in the history of Britain. Any town in command of a crossing of the Severn was bound to figure largely in any collision between Welsh and English, and the earldom and honour of Gloucester, obviously one of the great prizes for any lord, adhered usually to one of the princes of the blood.

Under Roman dominance, Gloucester was one of the very few British towns which were granted Roman civic rights, and the precision of the rectangular layout of the main streets still recalls the Roman mind. The great church which is now the cathedral dedicated to Holy Trinity was formerly the abbey church of the Benedictine monastery of St Peter, and became a cathedral and the head of a see after the Dissolution. But it had a long previous history as a religious foundation. The site began as a double monastery for Benedictines in the seventh century, for a time became a college for the secular clergy in the ninth, and then reverted to the Benedictines as the abbey of St Peter. About the end of the eleventh century the present church was begun by Abbot Serlo. Others following have embellished, restored and enlarged it with love, and the result is glorious.

After the Conquest it was King William's custom to wear his crown three times in the year, at his courts of Christmas, Easter and Whitsun, and the venue for Christmas was Gloucester. Whenever possible he held to this procedure. Great councils and parliaments were held here many times in the following centuries.

When Henry I died near Rouen, leaving only one legitimate child living – Maud, or Matilda, widow of the Emperor Henry V and married for the second time to Count Geoffrey of Anjou – the succession presented a problem, and gave rise to a long struggle between Maud, who had the handicap of being a woman, and Stephen, the dead king's nephew. Henry had induced his barons, during his lifetime, to swear fealty to Maud, but when Stephen rushed to claim the throne he carried everyone with him, and succeeded in getting himself crowned. But Maud took up the challenge, and as soon as she asserted her claim, and her father's wish

LEFT

The north transept and chapter house of Gloucester Cathedral, taken from the east.

to secure her succession, she gained, in Earl Robert of Gloucester, her most faithful and selfless supporter.

Robert was her half-brother, an illegitimate son of Henry I, and the embodiment of everything that was best in the Norman nobility. From the west country, from those very Marcher lands closest to Wales, he maintained his sister's right, and later her son's, until his death in 1147, from his bases in Gloucester and Bristol. He fought fair, he maintained law and peace, so far as that was possible, in the territories that came within his control, and once committed, he never swerved from his loyalty to the Empress, though with nothing to gain and much to lose.

Later the earldom passed at various times into the families of Audley, Clare and Despenser, and at other times was vested in members of the ruling house. The Clare earls took the side of the reform during the Barons' War, but Gilbert de Clare was finally the chief mover, next to Edward, in bringing about the fall and defeat of Simon de Montfort, by defecting to Edward's side and assisting him to escape from restraint by breaking his parole. After

Gloucester Cathedral's cloister range (built 1350–1412) and garden looking north-east.

Edward's victory, however, Gilbert did argue for reconciliation rather than revenge, and to his credit resisted the imposition of punitive measures against the defeated, while others were baying for their blood.

When held by a scion of the blood royal the title usually became duke rather than earl. Henry V's youngest brother, Humphrey, was Duke of Gloucester, and to me, at least, is an attractive character. He was a scholar and a patron of scholars, who not only loved and collected books, but also was generous with them, for on three occasions he gave books from his own library to an Oxford penurious and crying out for the means to scholarship. The traditional name of 'Duke Humphrey's Library' at Oxford still keeps his benefactions in remembrance. His political life was complex and troubled, his two marriages even more so, and his death almost certainly murder, by Suffolk, or at Suffolk's orders, in the turmoil of Henry VI's reign. But for bibliophiles and scholars his memory is to be reverenced, and perhaps it is not without reasonable cause that his Londoners called him their 'Good Duke Humphrey'.

Of the darker figure of the most celebrated of all dukes of Gloucester there is nothing to be said that has not been said before, in accusation or defence. Richard of Gloucester was certainly not guilty of quite all the crimes Shakespeare alleges against him, and it has been observed that during the life of his brother Edward IV he behaved with scrupulous correctness. But it is also on record that shortly after Edward died, leaving two male heirs of tender years, Richard suddenly discovered that the king to whom he had been so loyal was not legally married to his queen, and that his children were bastards, and therefore not legal heirs at all; whereas there was a brother ready to step into the vacancy. The theory was propounded by preaching friars of whom some, possibly inspired though hardly divinely, went one stage further, and stated that Edward himself had been illegitimate. Born abroad – who knew how he had been engendered? Brotherly loyalty and love had apparently died with King Edward. Other deaths were to follow.

But one royal death, more than a hundred and fifty years earlier, not only reflected great credit upon the city and the Benedictines of Gloucester, but brought in immense wealth in the offerings of pilgrims, and provided the means to glorify a glorious church still further. After the murder of Edward II at Berkeley castle in 1327,

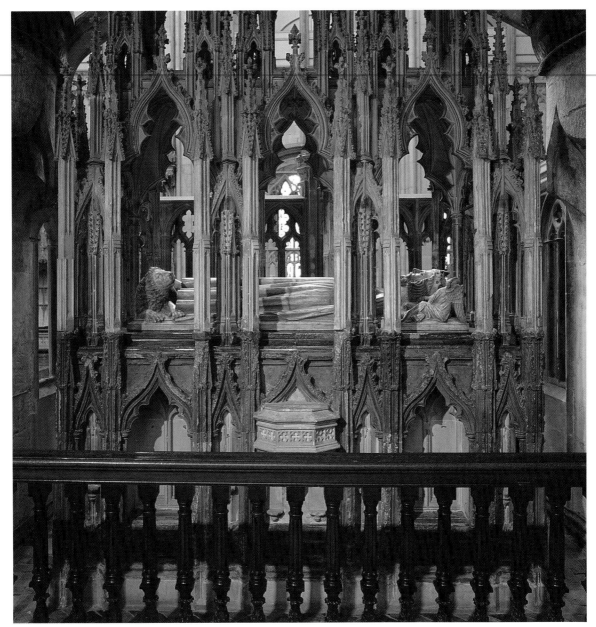

The tomb of Edward II at Gloucester Cathedral. This alabaster effigy on a tomb chest of Purbeck marble was made about 1330.

both Bristol and Malmesbury refused burial to the decomposing corpse, and every other religious house feared to take him in for dread of Queen Isabella and her lover Mortimer, who wielded complete power in the land. The abbot of St Peter's at Gloucester defied their threats, and with courage and compassion went to bring the wretched body home and give it not merely decent, but a glittering ceremonial burial in the abbey church. To the simple people of England the dead king, perhaps undeservedly but naturally enough in consideration of his misfortunes and dreadful death, gained the status of a martyr, and brought pilgrims to his tomb by the thousand. Their offerings maintained and beautified the church. So did his tomb effigy beautify it, for it is a wonderful work, and gave the dead king a resplendent comeliness and grace. The abbot's disinterested goodness can hardly have anticipated so rich a reward.

This monument to Elizabeth Williams, who died in 1622, is in the Lady Chapel of Gloucester Cathedral. It is one of the earliest church monuments to a commoner (i.e. not of royalty or clergy).

OVERLEAF

The Nomans called this the Golden Valley and so it remains, a landscape of wheat and apple orchards.

Golden Valley and Black Mountains

Upper Gwent, the district of Ewias, with its narrow north–south brook valleys and its grave, dark mountain ridges between, together with the rich arable and lush pasture of the region east of it, Erging to the Welsh, Archenfield to the English, shrouded itself in the same ambiguous duality as the rest of Gwent. Until the late twelfth century its culture and customs, and the saints it honoured in its church dedications, were predominantly Welsh. Saint Dyfrig is reputed to have been born in these parts, and his name proliferated in the patronage of parish churches. Norman encroachment here began early. By 1086 Ewias was an appanage of the house of Lacy, and Archenfield with its broad, sunlit pastures and rich soil was divided among a number of overlords, to whom their Welsh tenants paid their dues in honey, as once to their Welsh princes. A kind of midsummer glow seems to hang over the region, like a reflection of the name given to it, the Golden Valley. And here burst into flower the extraordinary style of carving known as the Herefordshire school, and best demonstrated by the church of Kilpeck, though echoes of its sinuous, intertwined Celtic shapes can be found on fonts and tympani well beyond the bounds of the county.

LEFT

These carvings are stone bosses from the now demolished nave of Abbey Dore.

Tretower Castle and Court

The splendid grouping of early Norman tower and ruins, and medieval manor-house, here in the south-eastern corner of Brecknock, was the chief seat of the honour of one of Bernard of Newmarch's principal vassals. The name simply means 'the village of the tower' the settlement obviously having grown up under the protection of the castle of the Picard family; though possibly the site had previously been fortified in some way by its Welsh lords. The name of Picard appears as a benefactor in the first charter in the cartulary of Brecon Priory, and the dynasty continued for many generations in possession here, and were generous patrons of the Benedictine monks of Brecon.

Later, in the fifteenth and sixteenth centuries, the manor-house was the home of the Vaughan family, and in particular of Henry Vaughan, one of the greatest of the seventeenth-century metaphysical poets.

Tretower Court is a fine example of a fifteenth-century manor-house, once the home of Henry Vaughan, poet.

Brecon

In the early stages of the Norman penetration into Wales, one of the Conqueror's enterprising barons, Bernard of Newmarch, established himself in the region of Brecknock, and built his main stronghold at the confluence of the Honddu and the Usk. He founded a borough there, known to his Welsh tenants as Aberhonddu, but the English called it Brecon after the lordship of which it was the capital. Bernard was a patron of the Conqueror's own abbey of Battle, and endowed that foundation with a part of the income of his borough to enable them to found a cell at Brecon. A monk of Battle visited him and received the grant of the church of St John, close to the castle, and the lands of the old Roman site a few miles to the west. The settlers from Battle rebuilt the church and added monastic quarters and brought in other brothers to establish Bernard's foundation. Bernard's wife gave the new house the manor of Berrington, near Tenbury, probably a part of her dowry, and the king sanctioned the inauguration of the priory of Brecon.

Brecon Cathedral stands on the site of a Benedictine Priory founded in 1093. The present cathedral was commenced in the thirteenth century and finished in the fourteenth century.

Longtown Castle

Situated only a few miles into Herefordshire under the eastern flank of the Black Mountains, almost midway between Llanthony Priory in Wales and Abbey Dore in England, Longtown presents an impressive stone ruin and a long street village which was surely intended to be a successful borough, but never quite made it. The castle belongs to the early Norman settlement, when hurried motte and bailey fortresses were frequent as bases along the border, but stone buildings of this massive construction rather rare. It must have been a matter for shrewd calculation where the strongest protection was needed, and Longtown may have been a miscalculation, for its name plays no part in the history of the Marches upon either side. Such sporadic troubles as it must have known in its day are gone into limbo, unrecorded.

OVERLEAF

High in the Black Mountains, above Llanthony Priory, this track leads down to Hay-on-Wye and is said to be the road that preachers took on their journeys into Wales, hence the name Pass of the Evangelist.

Abbey Dore

A Cistercian house, founded by the Norman Robert of Ewyas in the rich and beautiful Golden Valley of Herefordshire, Abbey Dore lived the troubled life of all border monasteries, but survived without major disaster until the Dissolution in 1536, though it was said to be somewhat neglected and ruinous in its later years as a monastery. What remains is the transepts and the vaulted aisled presbytery and ambulatory, in the green and gracious landscape that sets off stone so beautifully. The house had a valuable library, including its own annals up to the year 1362.

Abbey Dore is one of the few Cistercian churches in England still in use. Begun in 1180, the buildings fell to ruin at the time of the suppression in 1535 but were repaired in the mid-seventeenth century. The parts remaining today are the crossing, choir and ambulatory.

Kilpeck

The sculptured undulations of red Herefordshire earth set off the compact little church of Kilpeck on the skyline, the masterpiece of a renowned regional school of carving, known by the name of

Herefordshire but reaching over into neighbouring counties in small pleasures like the tympanum of Aston Eyre church in Shropshire, or the fonts at Stottesdon and Holdgate. But Kilpeck is the masterwork, with its sinuous, intertwined shapes and imaginative grotesques asserting a very strong individuality in the artist. The dating is Norman, but the influence is Celtic, a true expression of the Marches.

Pipton on the Wye

A detail of the left-hand jamb of the south doorway of Kilpeck Church showing what is believed to be a Welsh warrior on the inner shaft and serpents on the outer.

'I said that Llewelyn was no more than twenty miles from us, with the greater part of his force then mustered along the border. He was encamped at Pipton on the Wye, due west of Hereford by way of Hay, and he had with him there a good half of his council and several of his chief vassals, Rhys Fychan of Dynevor, and both the lords of Powys among them.'

'So much the better,' said Earl Simon, 'if he is attended in some splendour. This is what I would have you say to him.'

And he taught me such a message as uplifted my heart with joy and eagerness, and had me also write a letter which should expound his purpose, already in those few words made plain.

THE DRAGON AT NOONDAY

The message of Earl Simon de Montfort to Llewelyn ap Griffith, which brought about the meeting of envoys at Pipton, resulted in the Treaty of Pipton, sealed in June of 1265 between Henry III, then virtually a captive in the hands of the earl and his allies of the reform party, and the Prince of Wales. In the king's name Simon promised recognition of Llewelyn's title and right, with the homage of all the other Welsh princes, restoration of all lands taken at any time from Llewelyn's immediate predecessors, and the addition of the castles of Hawarden, Whittington and Painscastle. In return Llewelyn agreed to pay a high indemnity of 30,000 marks over ten years, and to maintain fealty to the king, as now, in the present government of the reform.

Thus strengthened, Earl Simon secured his position in South Wales without difficulty, took Monmouth, Usk and Newport, but found his crossing of the Severn everywhere barred by Prince

OVERLEAF

It is believed that a Saxon church preceded this one at Kilpeck, dating to the twelfth century. The church contains many fine carvings of the Herefordshire School which have been extremely well preserved.

Pipton on the Wye, where in 1265
Simon de Montfort, in the king's
name, acknowledged Llewelyn ap
Griffith's rights and titles.

Edward's army, and finally, after fording the river at Kempsey, was
brought to battle in very unfavourable circumstances at the fatal
field of Evesham. From then on, with Simon dead and the king
free to rule as he pleased, Llewelyn's sole aim was to extort from
Henry full ratification of the pledges and terms he had received
from the earl.

It took him somewhat over two years, but in September of
1267, at the Treaty of Montgomery, all the terms of the Treaty of
Pipton were ratified by King Henry.

Arthur's Stone, a prehistoric burial chamber (*c.* 3500 BC) in the hills above Bredwardine on the River Wye. It would originally have been covered with earth and have formed a mound.

There is no documentary evidence that Earl Simon de Montfort and Llewelyn ap Griffith actually met in person at Pipton, but in view of the fact that it must have been at this time that Simon betrothed his only daughter, Eleanor, to the prince, it seems reasonable to suppose that they did meet. At any rate, there is no positive proof to the contrary, and the matters to be discussed were important enough to need the most authoritative supervision. In particular, the betrothal must surely have been arranged between the parties most concerned; it was not a clause in the treaty. I like to think that two very great men met here in these river meadows, with the mountains of Wales looming to westward, and everything still to win or lose.

Arthur's Stone

This reptilian shape of stone near Dorstone in Herefordshire, is the inner chamber of a long barrow, the mound of which must have been some 18 metres long, and was oriented north–south. It dates from the New Stone Age. In Britain anything so antique and so mysterious must be associated with Arthur, and here, as in so many places, his name has attached itself to a phenomenon from the far-distant past. The same transference takes place in other lands, and with other heroes.

Hereford Cathedral

The canopied tomb of Peter of Aigueblanche (d. 1268) is in the north transept of Hereford Cathedral which he built. Beyond this tomb is the shrine to St Thomas Cantelupe who was Bishop between 1275 and 1282.

All the great cathedral cities of the March played a vital part in negotiations or hostilities between Welsh and English, as bases for both defence and attack, meeting places for discussion, for the signing of truce or the mustering of armies. Hereford, as the most westerly, was the most significant outpost of English power, and indeed provided the firm basis for the first Norman Earl of Hereford's gradual penetration of the whole of Gwent. But equally it was vulnerable to Welsh attack when grievances became intolerable or princes ambitious.

Its history in this border role goes back well beyond the coming of the Normans. In the year 926, King Athelstan called the leading Welsh princes to council in Hereford, and fixed the course of the Wye as the accepted boundary between the two peoples. In 760, obviously in less harmonious times, a battle between Welsh and English is recorded here. During the civil war between Stephen and the Empress Maud, contending for the Crown, the west, based strongly on Hereford, Bristol and Gloucester, was held for the Empress, and she revived the earldom of Hereford for her loyal supporter, Miles of Gloucester, and his son Roger, who succeeded him. Later the earldom came into the hands of the powerful Marcher family of Bohun.

The diocese of Hereford goes back to the year 680, and its bishops, like minor princes – sometimes, indeed, overruling kings – played a powerful part in Marcher history. During the Barons' War one of them, the Savoyard Peter of Aigueblanche, an unpopular and alien opponent of the Montfortian reform party, was seized and kept prisoner, and his manors raided by the impetuous young Marcher lords who were then Simon de Montfort's main adherents. He was reinstated later, and his tomb is in the north transept of the cathedral, where it shares the honour, ironically, with the later bishop, Thomas Cantelupe, who had been a firm supporter of the Provisions of Oxford, the ground of the reform movement, and a friend of Simon de Montfort. Bishop Thomas was a man of parts; he managed his diocese, very largely mismanaged during the rule of his predecessor, very ably, had been chancellor of Oxford University and a lecturer in canon law, and after the battle of

RIGHT

The Norman nave of Hereford Cathedral looking towards the west window. Rebuilding above the Norman columns and arches was carried out by the architect Wyatt in the nineteenth century.

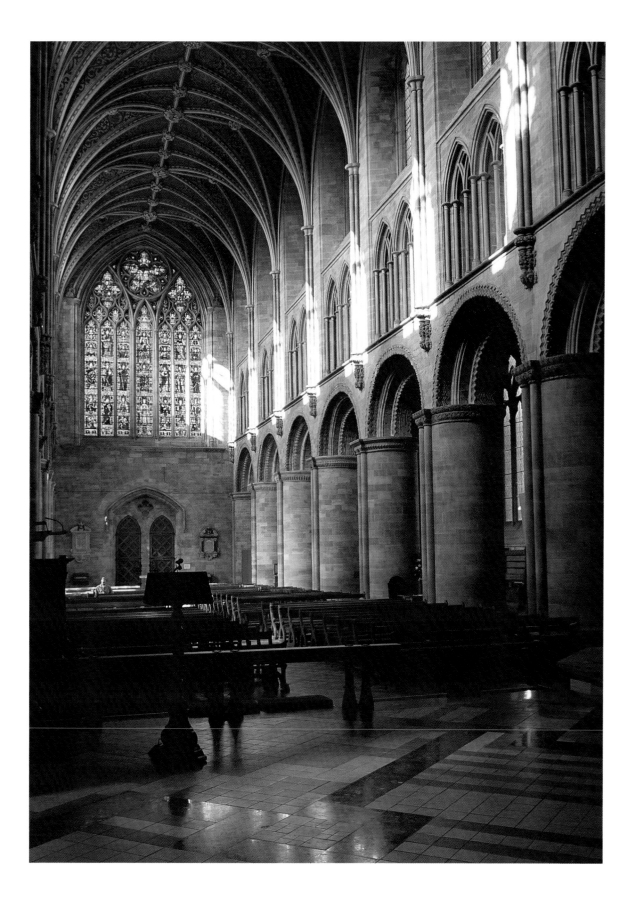

Standing on the banks of the River Wye near Hay, Clifford Castle is the place where 'Fair Rosamund' – Jane de Clifford – was born.

Lewes, when government was directed by Earl Simon in the king's name, served as chancellor of the kingdom. His integrity, as well as his ability, seems to have been the admiration of most men, though he did not get on at all well with the Archbishop of Canterbury, John Peckham, a much narrower man, a busy, bustling, officious reformer in a hurry. Peckham sought to arrogate to himself and his own court rights and cases which his bishops regarded as belonging to them, and much better left in their hands. Thomas was their spokesman, and Peckham's response was to excommunicate him, the fate of many an irreproachable soul both before and since his case. He promptly withdrew to the Pope in person at Orvieto to conduct his appeal, and was very warmly received. He died in Orvieto, and was temporarily buried there, until he was brought home to lie in the north transept of Hereford cathedral, set in train a chain of miracles, and became a saint. St Thomas Cantelupe is celebrated on the third day of October.

Clifford Castle

The first Norman castle here was one of the many built by the Earl of Hereford, William FitzOsbern, during the early years of the Conqueror's thrust to secure South Wales. The family into whose hands it later came took their name from the place, and became the powerful house of Clifford, with strong holdings in Herefordshire and the upper Wye.

Henry II's 'Fair Rosamund' lived here, lending her name to legend as a royal mistress. During the Barons' War, Roger Clifford was one of the young Marcher lords, contemporaries of the Lord Edward, who followed that prince for a time as enthusiastic supporters of Simon de Montfort's reform party. It was Clifford who led the raid that captured the unpopular Savoyard Bishop of Hereford, Peter of Aigueblanche, and imprisoned him in the castle of Eardisley. Later, when Edward abandoned Simon's cause to rally to the defence of the King, his father, he was able, almost inevitably, to win back all these young men with him. They were his generation, his friends, his own kind, almost his own household; they returned to his service and fought at Evesham against their, and his, former idol.

OVERLEAF

A view of the gentle hills and valleys near Llandrindod Wells in Mid-Wales.

The Landscape of Llewelyn's Death

In the region of the central March the destiny of Llewelyn ap Griffith and the fate of Wales were played out from triumph to final tragedy. In 1265, having won from the reformers recognition of all his rights and conquests, Llewelyn had escorted Simon de Montfort's army towards the crossing of the river at Kempsey, and the fatal defeat of Evesham, but he continued to retain his position until he won the same acknowledgement from the king after that battle, when King Henry's control of his government was fully re-established. The year 1267 saw the pinnacle of Llewelyn's power and sovereignty. Fifteen years later, and many miles due west of that same ford at Kempsey, in the final war of 1282 against the full power of England under Edward I, the prince came south from his beleaguered stronghold of Gwynedd to recruit support from the princes of Builth and Elfael, and in a comparatively limited circle of the most remote and secret uplands of central Wales he met his death in a disorderly battle tainted by rumours of treachery. The place of his death and the place of his burial mark the end of the ancient tribal Wales, and the frustration of the concept of a Wales at last united, a national feudal state. On the frontier between the triumph and the tragedy, the lovely magpie villages of the fringes of Herefordshire radiate well-being and peace.

Nearly all houses in the village of Pembridge are built of timber, and this bell tower is no exception. It was built in the thirteenth century and is supported by massive oak columns and beams.

Aberedw

*L*ewelyn had a little castle at Aberedw, south of Builth, that he had used formerly as a hunting lodge, and though it was on the eastern side of the Wye, it was still secure, and as an intelligence base for an army, to be used and quitted as best served, it was excellent. There the prince took up his headquarters for a time, while we probed the state of feeling in the country round, and found friends enough, though they went in fear of the king's men, and reported Builth castle as impregnable, a judgement we accepted.

When we came there, young Edmund Mortimer had still not received seisin of his father's lands, though it was granted at last about the twenty-fourth of November, and both the young men were said to be much affronted by the delay, and not at all unsympathetic to the Welsh among their tenants, even though they knew these men willed victory to the prince. In some degree, to be a Marcher baron was to understand the passion for land, the sense of sovereign lordship, as kings were unable to do, who lived by overlordship, and desired to suppress that identity with land that such as Mortimer truly felt, and reduce them to mere custodians for the Crown.

AFTERGLOW AND NIGHTFALL

In the last stages of the war of 1282 Llewelyn had gone south into the region of Builth to try and raise further allies, while his brother David held the position in the north as well as he could. Not far from here, where the little River Edw empties into the Wye under these rocks, Llewelyn was killed in the last throes of a fight that had decimated his forces in his absence, a local man having betrayed to the English a secret ford which enabled them to cross the river undetected and surround the Welsh, who had expected attack only by the bridge. After Llewelyn's death David, so long uncertain in his loyalties, assumed the burden his brother had left behind, and carried it faithfully to its tragic end.

LEFT

There is a cave called Llewelyn's Cave in these rocks at Aberedw which is said to be the place where he spent his last night.

Not far to the west of Builth Wells at Cilmery (Cefn-y-Bedd Llewelyn) stands this stone monument to Llewelyn ap Griffith.

Cefn-y-Bedd Llewelyn: The Ridge of Llewelyn's Grave

They say he was still breathing, and lived some few minutes more, when Lestrange's men found him and knew him at last. If so, they must have come very soon after I left him. I let fall the broken shaft out of my hand, and turned and went stumbling and groping up the slope towards the forest, fleeing that field of Orewin Bridge as once I fled the field of Evesham, and leaving, as then, a great piece of my own being dead beside the body of a man I loved and revered above all others. And I cried silently to God in the darkness of my spirit and the darkness of the night, as I had cried for Earl Simon, that in this world there was no justice, but the best were calumniated and betrayed and brought to nought, as God himself was when he ventured among the sons of men.

AFTERGLOW AND NIGHTFALL

This stark and moving memorial marks the approximate location of Llewelyn ap Griffith's first hasty burial, after the battle close by Builth, before his body was taken to Abbey Cwm Hir.

Kempsey

In the evening and night of the second of August we forded the Severn opposite the manor of Kempsey, making down to the water where there was cover from willows. Some of Bishop Walter's people had been on the watch for us, and stood by to show the best passage. The water was still high enough, but leisurely in its flow, and the bottom firm and smooth, without hazards. A slow business it was, but accomplished before dawn, and at Kempsey we had some rest before the sun rose, for the bishop's household was staunch like its master, and willing to take risks for the earl's cause.

THE DRAGON AT NOONDAY

This was in the year 1265, when Simon de Montfort, with King Henry in his care, was facing the final battle to preserve the reforms enshrined in the Provisions of Oxford. His army was on the Welsh side of the Severn, and all the river bridges held strongly against him, and his objective was to cross and reach Kenilworth, where he hoped his son, Simon the Younger, would join him with reinforcements. Bishop Walter Cantelupe of Worcester had been throughout a staunch supporter of the reforms, and at his holding of Kempsey, in this quiet spot on the Severn, Simon's army forded the river. But Edward, who was at Worcester, intercepted the expected force from the south, and the army of the reform got no further than Evesham. On 4 August the final and fatal battle was fought there, and Earl Simon died on the battlefield.

Of the bishops who had supported the cause of the reform throughout, Bishop Walter died early in the following year, before their fate was determined, but the bishops of London, Lincoln, Chichester and Winchester were all suspended from their office and ordered to the papal court. Only one was allowed to return and resume his office. One died in exile in Viterbo; the remaining two waited seven years before they were allowed back to England.

Kempsey church stands on the bank of the Severn where Simon de Montfort made his crossing on his way to the battle at Evesham.

Villages of the Herefordshire Border

The spectacular black and white settlements of the Herefordshire March, Eardisley, Eardisland, Pembridge, Weobley, almost all of them with at least the green motte of a former castle somewhere close by, are at once a witness to a stormy past, and a triumphant survival to a peaceful and beautiful present. The black and white of Herefordshire is the early, plain rectangular and linear style, without fanciful elaboration, but ever-present, a gay, pied frontage of dwellings against the lushest and most fertile of countrysides. An elegant eccentricity like the massive detached bell tower of the church at Pembridge suffices to provide an instant of surprise and a vertical accent in this fantasy of timber beams stressing so strongly the horizontal.

An old timber-framed cottage at Eardisland by the side of the River Arrow.

Cefnllys

In the year 1262, at a time of prolonged truce between England and Llewelyn ap Griffith of Wales, when new castle building was prohibited by the terms of the agreement, Roger Mortimer, Llewelyn's cousin and opponent, moved westward from Wigmore into Welsh territory, and began to build or rebuild a castle on the crest of this ridge of Cefnllys, a couple of miles east of the modern Llandrindod Wells, and a great many miles west of the English border. The men of Maelienydd, alarmed and angry, took the law into their own hands, drove out the builders, and burned the rising castle. Roger mustered an army, supported by his neighbour Humphrey de Bohun, and returned to the site, encamping there in force within what was left of his perimeter wall to protect the masons while they worked. The local Welsh, unable to compete with such numbers, sent to ask Llewelyn for help. He came in strength, and laid siege to the intruding force, shutting them tightly within the shell of the castle and cutting off supplies.

It was plain that they had only limited supplies, and that they were advanced so far from Mortimer's base at Wigmore as to be very badly placed for breaking out of our trap, all those miles of hostile Maelienydd separating them from reinforcements. We could starve them into submission in a week or two. But Llewelyn had a better use for those seven days.

'Now let's see,' he said, 'how practical a man Roger can be. For he knows his situation as well as we do, and I think has the good sense to recognize and admit it. I have no great ambition to fight with him, and I would as lief have him out of here and out of my way while I secure Maelienydd.'

He told us what he proposed, and David laughed and begged to be the ambassador to the besieged. He rode into the enclosure attended by a single squire, and laid before Roger Mortimer, no doubt with a demure and dignified face, the prince's offer. Since it was clear that surrender was only a matter of time, and relief exceedingly improbable, why expend men and resources in postponing the inevitable? Llewelyn had no wish to fight with his cousin. If Mortimer would accept it, he and his army were offered free and unimpeded passage through Llewelyn's lines and across the border, intact to a man, with all their gear.

OVERLEAF

The hill at Cefnllys where in 1262 Roger Mortimer began to rebuild an old castle. It is possible there was a fort on this hill in pre-Roman times.

That was no easy decision to make, but Mortimer was a big enough man, and honest enough with himself, to shrug off what many a younger and rasher captain would have seen as disgrace and dishonour. Indeed, later he was plagued with suggestions in many quarters that he had been in league with the Welsh in this matter, which I can testify was quite false. He could have stayed and fought, and seen many of his men wounded and killed, only to surrender in the end. Instead, he chose to take his whole force home in good order when he was given the chance. For my part, I respect his commonsense, and so, I think, must the wives of his soldiers have done when their men came home unmarked.

We opened our ranks to let them out, and saluted them as they marched by, for we had nothing against them, and the message they were taking back to King Henry was more galling than a bloody defeat would have been.

'I call that good housekeeping,' said Llewelyn, watching their ranks recede towards Knighton. 'We've spent little to gain much, and he's preserved what could be preserved. No fool squandering of men for spite or stubbornness, as your thickheaded heroes would have done. I approve him.'

THE DRAGON AT NOONDAY

A natural defensive site, Cefnllys bears along its crest signs of an early hill-fort, and the remains of two separate castles, so this encounter in 1262 may have been an attempt to replace or enlarge an earlier fortress fallen into disuse because of Welsh gains in the region.

Abbey Cwm Hir

The final burial place of Llewelyn ap Griffith, remote in the valley of the Clywedog Brook, north of Llandrindod Wells.

And for that dear body, it rests headless, like Earl Simon's body, felon and saint, yet it rests, in the unrelenting memories of men as in the gentle earth. The young chaplain kept his word, and reported faithfully to Dame Maud Giffard the news of her cousin's death, and before worse slight could be put upon his person she sent and had the corpse delivered with all reverence into the care of the Cistercian brothers of Cwm Hir Abbey, and forthwith wrote to Archbishop Peckham, requesting absolution for Llewelyn,

that he might be buried in consecrated ground. Peckham replied, and duly notified Edward that he had so replied, that he could not without sin do as she asked unless she produced proof that the prince had shown sign of penitence before he died. Whereupon she showed that he had asked for a priest, and that her priest had indeed ministered to him. And further, Edmund Mortimer testified that his servants, present on the field, had also borne witness that the prince had made confession to a priest, while his brother Roger said that a Cistercian had sung Mass for the prince the day he died, and the furnishings of his chapel, and the vestments, were in Roger's care, and could be seen.

So they spoke for him, and they prevailed, and he is buried in blessedness at Cwm Hir, in a spot so remote and fair and still, they who are laid there cannot but rest well.

And for these reasons here set out, I absolve the Mortimers of that cruel treachery that slew Llewelyn and stripped Wales of its shield and sword. And I am glad, as he is glad, where he abides. For they were his kin, and he had a kindness for them.

AFTERGLOW AND NIGHTFALL

An abbey was built here at Abbey Cwm Hir in the twelfth century. Among these ruins there is a modern slate memorial tablet to Llewelyn ap Griffith, who was probably buried here.

OVERLEAF

A view of the fertile farmland from Richard's Castle.

The Land of the Mortimers

The central March of Wales was dominated for more than four centuries by the powerful house of Mortimer. As early as 1075 the first of the dynasty, Ralph Mortimer I, was endowed by William the Conqueror with a number of manors in Shropshire and Herefordshire, and made the caput of his honour at Wigmore. From there his heirs extended their lands into Wales, until at the height of their glory their palatine extended from Cleobury and Leintwardine in the east to the limits of Maelienydd and Gwerthrynion in the west, and from Chirk in the north to the bounds of Elfael in the south. They held castles at Radnor, Knucklas, Cefnllys and other places in the central uplands of Wales, intermarried with the princely houses of Gwynedd and Powys, and were as often in alliance with them as fronting them in arms, quite a normal complication in border territory.

Beyond their actual holding in lands, which was immense, and eventually justified the title of Earls of March, they produced a succession of powerful personalities who inevitably played a major part in English and Welsh history. For a century, spanning four generations, they were the legitimate heirs to the English throne, and finally achieved it for a brief period of twenty-four years. The claim began with the nomination by Richard II, who had no son to succeed him, of Roger Mortimer as his heir presumptive. Roger was already known publicly as such at the parliament of Shrewsbury in 1398, for he was hailed as the heir by the populace, by whom it seems he was very well liked. The usurpation of Henry IV intervened to prevent his line from acceding, but his claim was not forgotten. It erupted in several abortive conspiracies, until Edward, Earl of March, finally became Edward IV. With the death of his brother, Richard III, and the arrival of the Tudors, the house of Mortimer withdraws from the ambience of royalty, but the echo of the name still rings resoundingly across the central March.

LEFT

Richard's Castle is named after the Norman, Richard FitzScrob, who built a castle here before the Conquest. It is probable that he founded the church of St Bartholomew next to the castle remains.

Leominster Priory

Now used as the parish church, Leominster Priory was previously a monastic building of the Benedictine order; it contains examples of church building from many periods.

The small Benedictine priory of Leominster was dedicated to Sts Peter and Paul. In times of discord between Wales and England its lands were vulnerable to Welsh raiding. There is a letter of Llewelyn the Great, probably dated around 1230, to his bailiffs of Maelienydd, warning them not to interfere with the priory. Llewelyn respected the Benedictine order, though his own preference was for the Cistercian houses.

Thomas Cantelupe, Bishop of Hereford, later canonized, once visited Leominster and found that the prior had locked the door of the church against the townspeople, although it was also the parish church. He ordered the door to be removed bodily, leaving worshippers free to enter. Archbishop John Peckham, who visited the house after the bishop's death, was scandalized to see the monks exposed to public view, and promptly had the door replaced. But he caused an additional chapel to be added for parish use.

The Church at Pilleth

He withheld the signal until the range was close enough to be deadly, and the stocky Welsh ponies were stretching their frenzied necks and rigid nostrils for the impact, and then flung up his arm, and waited for the tremendous thrumming in the air, that maddening, intoxicating sound like a thousand wild geese all taking flight at once.

It did not come. The volley of arrows was thin and broken, its unevenness jangling in his nerves even before his senses recorded it. He turned, incredulous, to stare, and saw half his array of bowmen, the Welsh-born half, standing mute and grim with bows on shoulders, some slowly raising them, some fitting the shafts, and he knew, by their faces and their movements, where those shafts were bound. He uttered a great cry of anger and shame, without words, and then the words came following, so hotly that they burned in his throat:

'Traitors – traitors! You've eaten my salt and taken my pay . . . !'

But they were Welsh! He should have foreseen it. Mercenary soldiers are mercenary only skin-deep, they still have blood, and the blood can out-argue the indentures and the oaths of fealty sworn for pay. In his heart, even as the first shaft sliced into the flesh of his left arm, he did not really blame them.

A BLOODY FIELD BY SHREWSBURY

Beneath this hillside where the small church stands, in the meadows of the valley of the River Lugg, was fought the battle of Pilleth, where Edmund Mortimer, the Mortimer of Shakespeare's *King Henry IV*, ran full tilt into a fighting company led by Owen Glendower, and was betrayed by the Welsh archers of his household troops, who turned their shafts upon his Englishmen rather than fire on the Welsh prince. Mortimer was wounded and captured, and left to lie captive by the king, who had all too many dynastic reasons for wanting all the Mortimers out of the way. Henry's refusal even to countenance the ransom of Edmund was a substantial part of the reason why Hotspur turned against him, and the main reason why Mortimer, left in Welsh hands, married Glendower's daughter and adopted the prince's cause. The battle that took place beneath these peaceful border hills led eventually to the battle of Shrewsbury, King Henry's shaky salvation, and the death of Hotspur.

Pilleth church stands on a hill overlooking the meadows of the River Lugg, the slaying fields of 1401.

Wigmore Castle

Wigmore was one of William FitzOsbern's early castles, the chief outpost of English power in the central March. When William's successor was foolish enough to enter into a conspiracy against the king, and was imprisoned for life, and the earldom of Hereford abolished for the foreseeable future, the king bestowed Wigmore and its duties and privileges in the March upon Ralph Mortimer, along with a number of manors in the region, including Cleobury and Leintwardine. Ralph was the first of the tremendous line of Mortimers who played such a tempestuous part in England's history for centuries.

When Henry II became king, and set about restoring order in a country that had survived years of chaos through civil war, he had trouble in suppressing some of his recalcitrant barons, including Hugh Mortimer of Wigmore. Henry had to capture the castles of Cleobury and Bridgnorth, as well as the chief seat of the honour, before Hugh submitted and made his peace.

The Roger Mortimer of Edward I's Welsh wars was first cousin to his great rival Llewelyn ap Griffith, fought against him stoutly for England, but also seems to have respected him, and won his respect. Such relationships resulted from the tangle of inter-Marcher and mixed Welsh–English marriages that were so frequent in the twelfth and thirteenth centuries. Roger's two young sons, Edmund and Roger, bore witness, after Llewelyn's death, that he had asked for a priest before dying, and that he had heard Mass on the day of his death, and had his chaplain and the instruments of grace with him in the field, and so helped to procure for him burial in holy ground and with the proper rites. Maud Clifford, another cousin, since her mother was another daughter of Llewelyn the Great, had the prince reverently buried at Abbey Cwm Hir. Enemies could be close kin, and behave at times more like kin than enemies.

The names of Roger and Edmund alternate in the Mortimer dynasty. The grandson of Llewelyn's cousin-enemy, another Roger, made the name notorious and hated as the lover and fellow-conspirator of Edward II's Queen Isabella, Gray's 'she-wolf of France'. Certainly Edward had brought his own credit low enough to provoke anger and hatred in his subjects, both high and low, but his consort and her lover went to extremes of which his weaker nature was incapable. They deposed and imprisoned him, and finding he still had friends enough to attempt his rescue, inevitably resorted to the final solution usual in such cases, and had him brutally murdered. For a time Isabella and Mortimer, or more probably Mortimer through Isabella, ruled England, until the young king, Edward III, was old enough to strike out boldly on his own account, rid himself of Mortimer, and pension off his mother into

OVERLEAF

Wigmore Castle was the most impressive castle in the middlemarch, home of the most powerful of the Marcher lords – the Mortimers.

a far too liberal retirement. She was his mother, he could not contemplate bringing about her death. Even in the legal presentation of the case, he suppressed all mention of her liaison, laying the blame only on Mortimer, officially for intriguing to turn her against her husband, the king.

Edward showed balance and generosity in dealing with the Mortimer family. The sins of the father were not visited upon the children. Roger's son Edmund died within a year of his father's fall, leaving a small boy, another Roger, as his heir. The earldom of March, which had been claimed by Isabella's lover during their dominance, lay in abeyance, but was ultimately restored by King Edward when the child grew up, and distinguished himself in loyal service to the Crown during the French wars. Another Edmund followed, and another Roger.

This Roger was important, and even after his early death in 1398 played havoc with English history. For the then king Richard II, having no son to succeed him, had been urged to name his chosen successor, and with general agreement had named Roger Mortimer, Earl of March. As it fell out, Roger died before the king himself was challenged, deposed and done away with by Henry of Bolingbroke, who proceeded by devices dubious indeed in law and questionable in parliamentary procedure, to make himself King Henry IV.

Roger, Earl of March, legitimate heir or not, was dead, and could hardly speak up for his own right, but he had left behind three living male heirs and one little daughter, plus a sister who, if all other claimants failed, had the right by precedent to be considered their heiress; and she was married to Henry Percy of Northumberland, history's incandescent Harry Hotspur, and had borne him a son, also Henry. Altogether, even if the named successor by law was dead, still six people stood, legally, between Henry IV and the crown he had usurped.

The Percys had supported him, and fully acknowledged the wrongs Henry had suffered at Richard's hands. The king probably had no anxieties where they were concerned, at least during his first years in power. But the two little boys Roger had left behind, as usual named Edmund and Roger, and the dead earl's younger brother, also Edmund, and the little girl Anne, were a very different matter. The new king took care to place the children safely in the care of close adherents of his own. The young man Edmund, left in temporary tenure of the Mortimer borderlands, was kept at arm's length, and showed no sign of giving trouble. Not yet. And perhaps he never would have thought of giving trouble if he had not set out to fight off a Welsh raid in the valley of the Lugg, had his own Welsh archers turn traitor, and been captured and carried off prisoner by the henchmen of Owen Glendower, self-declared and very formidable prince of Wales.

It was the king's refusal to provide, or even permit, the ransom of Mortimer which tipped the scale for the Percys. Hotspur valued his wife's brother, and confidently expected Henry to pay up to reclaim him, or at least allow his relatives to raise the ransom for him. Henry's refusal, seeing he already had the children in his hands, and now was patently glad to get rid of their uncle, was quite enough to arouse suspicions of what might happen should there be any sign of a faction forming to support the Mortimer claim. In fact, Henry probably created the very situation he feared, for the Mortimer clan did indeed rise to confront him, and even to survive him, to surface again, time after time, in the years that followed.

The immediate result was the revolt of the three powerful allies who, according to Shakespeare, planned to depose Henry and divide all England and Wales between them: Owen Glendower, bent on regaining Wales; Edmund Mortimer, by this time married to Glendower's daughter and to Glendower's cause no less; and the Percys of Northumberland. Their plans were shattered at the battle of Shrewsbury in 1403, when King Henry moved with uncharacteristic speed, and was able to bring the Percys to the field before Glendower and Mortimer could arrive to assist them.

But the claim of the earls of March was by no means dead. It surfaced in the Southampton Plot against Henry V, to do away with the king and his brothers and put the Mortimer Earl of March on the throne, in belated justice, and it broke into an active challenge in the Yorkist cause in the Wars of the Roses. For Anne Mortimer had married Richard, Earl of Cambridge, son of the Duke of York, and their son was Richard of York. In the male line Richard derived any claim he had by descent from Edward III's fourth son, which still left the usurper Henry IV ahead of him, Henry's father being the third son. But to this was added his claim through his mother, Anne Mortimer, through descent from the second son through Philippa, daughter of Lionel, Duke of Clarence. The two factions, Lancaster and York, stood on their real or supposed rights, to fight out the bloody battle that went back and forth between red rose and white, dealing slaughter impartially either way, and finally ushering in, ironically, the Welsh house of Tudor.

After that the name of Mortimer recedes into the blanket of the dark, and Wigmore, after four hectic centuries at the heart of history, gradually moulders into the gaunt and solitary ruin it is today.

Richard's Castle

The castle which gave its name to this small ancient borough predates the Conquest by about sixteen years, though it was thoroughly Norman. Edward the Confessor, more Norman than English, encouraged the settlement of Norman kinsmen and friends in Herefordshire, and gave them lavish gifts of land. This plot a few miles south-west of Ludlow was a grant to Richard FitzScrob, who built himself a strong castle on it about 1050, further elevating the hilltop and bedrock with earth on which to site his keep. The church of St Bartholomew was added within the defences, probably in his or his son's time in its first form, to serve the inhabitants of the borough that grew up under the shadow of the castle. Apparently there was some resistance among the English lords to these incursions of Norman landholders, for an attempt was made to persuade the king to expel the Frenchmen gathered in Richard's fortress, but the demand was refused. A year or so later there was an order made to expel the French, but people in the king's favour were excluded, Richard FitzScrob among them. The castle continued in his line for several generations before it passed by marriage to the family of Talbot, under the overlordship of the Mortimers.

By Leland's survey of 1540 the castle is reported as still mainly standing, but ruinous, and later it housed a farm and its buildings, with a dovecote in one of the towers. The property passed through several hands before coming finally into the possession of the Salwey family, which continued to hold it for 370 years.

A view of St Bartholomew's church and the Herefordshire countryside from the motte of Richard FitzScrob's ruined castle.

The church of St Bartholomew, enlarged in the fourteenth century, has a separate bell-tower as strong as a castle keep, clearly designed for defence. The whole group, on its lofty site, remote without any oppressive feeling of solitude, and with a few neighbouring houses around a minute green, is very impressive and warmly attractive, with wonderful views over the rich Herefordshire countryside.

Ludlow

The pivotal stronghold of the entire March, Ludlow was a planned town from the early years after the Conquest, the three main elements of any ambitious plantation deployed along a commanding ridge – the castle at the steep west end, with the river Teme coiling below its wooded cliff, the church at the east end, and the wide market-place stretching all along the ridge between, later busily colonized into a maze of narrow lanes, to the considerable enhancement of its charms. The castle was a possession of the de Lacy family, earls of Lincoln from 1233 to 1348 by marriage to a niece of Ranulf de Blundeville, who died childless. Later, during the Wars of the Roses, Ludlow was one of the family homes of Richard of York, and a strong base of the Yorkist cause. In October 1459, at the battle of Ludford Bridge on the edge of the town, York's forces were defeated, his town and castle plundered, and he himself forced to take refuge for a time in Ireland, while his son Edward, afterwards Edward IV, reached France by way of Devon.

Ludlow Castle and the tower of St Laurence's church seen from Whitcliffe. The church was founded some time before 1199 but most of the building dates from the late fourteenth and early fifteenth centuries. The castle was started about 1085 by, it is presumed, Roger de Montgomery, Earl of Shrewsbury.

The Yorkists returned, of course, as soon as they felt strong enough, to win at Northampton and lose at Wakefield, where Richard of York died, leaving the entire inherited claim of the Mortimers to be carried by Edward, Earl of March.

In this warfare the Marcher barons and even the Welsh were divided, since the Yorkist cause was the inherited and patently legal claim of the Mortimers, but Henry VI had loyal Welsh adherents, since the Tudor clan were kin to him, for the king's mother, early widowed by the death of Henry V, had secretly married a Tudor and had sons by him. The course of events was further entangled by the changing loyalties of powerful men like the Earl of Warwick. But, eventually, after the battle of Tewkesbury, the descendant of the Mortimers did secure the throne as Edward IV.

When Edward IV died, on 9 April 1483, the new child-king Edward V was in residence at Ludlow castle with his younger brother. They set out for London towards the end of the month, to a coronation, but were diverted by Richard of Gloucester into the Tower, and to their deaths.

It was Edward IV who first created the Council of the Marches, with its headquarters at Ludlow. The castle became the residence and court of the Lord President, an office filled for some twenty-seven years by Sir Henry Sidney, father of Sir Philip Sidney. The dwelling range of buildings within the castle enclosure dates from his years of office, and his son, the darling of the Elizabethans, spent much of his boyhood with Ludlow as his home, and attended school in Shrewsbury. Later, when the Earl of Bridgewater became Lord President, his arrival was celebrated in the great hall of the castle by the performance of Milton's masque of 'Comus', with the poet present, and Henry Lawes, the composer of the music, conducting the musicians.

Splendidly medieval and urbanely Georgian, Ludlow is an extremely beautiful town, and the surrounding countryside is equally lovely.

OVERLEAF

Near this spot, on the River Severn at Cressage, St Augustine is said to have preached below an oak tree. This would explain why at the time of Domesday the place was called Cristesache or Christ's Oak.

The Banks of Severn

In every border region between ethnic rivals the rivers play a vital and often decisive role. In the southern March it is the Wye that controls movements and limits fields of action. Further north it is the Severn, and the country watered and drained by the Severn, a rich and ample land of tributary floodplains and sheltering hills, softening as the river flows north, before turning away eastward, and quitting the border scene for a long detour into unquestionably English territory, until it veers westward and touches Wales again, opening out into its broad estuary below Chepstow. The northward course of the river from Caersws to Welshpool and the Breiddens is dotted with castles and the mottes of old castles for miles on either side, Clun and Hopton and Caus to the east, Mathrafal and Caerinion and Carreghofa to the west, and almost within sight of each other either side of the river, the royal rock of Montgomery and Llewelyn's last castle of Dolforwyn, last to be built and first to be abandoned, a source of contention with the town of Montgomery, because the burgesses feared for their market with a rival borough so near. Commercial hostilities, no less than land hunger, could feed fuel into border wars.

A mile or so from Montgomery itself the ford of Rhyd Chwima, in a green, neglected solitude now, marks the place where once an agreed peace was made between east and west, complaints heard, wrongs righted, and a Prince of Wales formally acknowledged. Downriver the town of Welshpool and the vanished monastery of Strata Marcella guard the Welsh shore, and inland, on the English, beyond the barrier of the Long Mountain, monastic splendour in ruins, Cluniac, Cistercian and Augustinian, and the noble remains of two ambitious houses of merchant and bishop-chancellor ornament the gracious valleys of Shropshire.

Hopton Castle

This formidable ruined keep in the extreme south-west of Shropshire is old enough in foundation, strong enough, and certainly looks grim enough to have played a desperate and perilous part in the history of Norman relations with Wales at least from the time of Henry II and possibly earlier. Close neighbour to the Welsh of Powys, it must have seen sporadic raiding in its time, yet recorded history has passed it by until the Civil War, when it was garrisoned for Parliament, besieged by the Royalist forces for three weeks, and refused an offer of honourable quarter in return for surrender, preferring to fight to the last man. Every man of the garrison was killed and the castle slighted and abandoned. Several Shropshire castles suffered similar treatment, for the county was fairly evenly

The Norman keep – all that is left of Hopton Castle.

divided between Royalists and Cromwellians; but these wounds were no part of the inevitable racial collisions of the Marches, but Englishmen tearing Englishmen.

Stokesay

The gatehouse to Stokesay Castle, one of the earliest fortified houses in England (1270–80), is late sixteenth century.

One of the earliest and boldest of fortified manor-houses in Britain, the most triumphant survivor and the most ravishing domestic grouping, Stokesay is unique. We call it a castle, perhaps in the sense that an Englishman's home is his castle. For this was the dream-house of no baron, but a wealthy wool merchant, Laurence of Ludlow, who took a lovely green valley site with the remnant of one stone tower, and built on a great hall, and later another handsome show tower at the further end. If he designed it himself, he had an artist's eye and a stout yeoman's confidence in his own ability to stand up for himself, for he built his hall with man-high windows, both within and without, surrounded it with only a decorative wall and moat, and probably hypnotized whoever owned and farmed the fields to westward into organizing the large, tranquil pond across which it is now so frequently photographed. The church, an integral part of the grouping which must then have been part-Saxon, part-Norman, has since been restored mainly in the seventeenth century, but it conforms to the atmosphere of the whole. So does the almost unbelievable gatehouse, stone below, seventeenth-century timber-framed above, exuberant with carvings.

The gem has been preserved in the amber of loving care. English Heritage nurses it, and inspired custodians look after it, cherish grass and gardens within the wall and keep the moat blossoming, fruitful and mown. People succumb to Stokesay.

Clun Castle

In the extreme south-west corner of Shropshire, fronting the hills of Welsh Kerry and Maelienydd, Clun was clearly a vulnerable settlement, and needed a strong castle to command the approaches from the west. Up to the coming of the Normans this corner of the shire was wholly rural, and settled as much by Welshmen as by the

Of Norman origin, Clun Castle was built above the River Clun, guarding a broad valley route into Wales.

English, very much like the north-west salient of Oswestry, where this frontier situation was duplicated. Soon after the Conquest castles were begun at both, and building in stone must in both cases have followed as soon as possible afterwards, together with the planting of the town. The river that gives Clun its name folds virtually round three sides of the castle site. For much of the period of the High Middle Ages both Clun and Oswestry were held by the FitzAlans, and both settlements suffered from sporadic raids and occasional destruction by fire. At the same time both retained their Anglo-Welsh character, and were meeting-places for both peoples as well as vulnerable to battles between the two.

Much Wenlock Priory

Royally founded, and twice refounded, each time with a different dedication, the impressive sculptural shapes of Wenlock's ruins are among the most beautiful monastic remains in the Marches. The first convent on these green grounds was a nunnery founded by King Merewald of Mercia about the year 680, for his daughter Milburga, who became its prioress and patron saint. Almost two hundred years later the nunnery was burned by the Danes.

The second foundation on the same ground came about 1050, when Earl Leofric of Mercia built here a minster, possibly for secular canons. Then the Normans came, and the Conqueror's friend and kinsman Roger de Montgomery became Earl of Shrewsbury in 1070, and ten years later appealed to the Abbot of Cluny to send over monks to serve the church, and turned it into an alien priory and daughter of Cluny's eldest daughter, La Charité on the Loire, from which the original band of monks came. Under such patronage the priory flourished. It became denizen, severing the link with Cluny in 1395, and thus was relieved of the heavy dues levied on alien priories, though it had to make a down payment to the exchequer for its freedom.

In 1101 the Cluniac monks discovered the burial place of the first prioress, St Milburga, and Archbishop Anselm allowed the bones to be reverently washed and encased in a new shrine, to continue their former tale of miracles.

The compact block of the former infirmary and prior's lodging survive as one of the most beautiful dwelling-houses conceivable, its frontage a two-storeyed screen of windows under a great single steep of stone-slated roof.

The little town that grew up on the skirts of the priory, built mainly of local stone, matches the beauty of the monastic ruins.

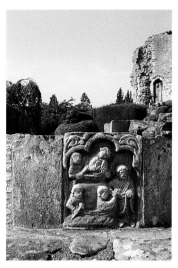

A detail from the twelfth-century lavatorium at Wenlock Priory. The panel shows Christ on the lake.

The Castle of Montgomery

The first Norman castle here was built by Roger de Montgomery, Earl of Shrewsbury, and named after his ancestral seat in Normandy. It is not certain whether the actual site was the formidable ridge of rock where the later fortress was built, or the mound of Hen Domen close by, though the fact that it was captured by the Welsh shortly afterwards and held for various periods in the years

OVERLEAF

There has been a religious house on this site since the seventh century. The ruins of Wenlock Priory are, in the main, from the twelfth century.

that followed suggest it was less daunting than the building that followed.

After a number of Welsh–English clashes in 1223 the government of the young Henry III decided to take the lordship of
Montgomery into Crown possession, and build up the castle into a
border fortress of great strength, and the erection of the stone castle
on the rocky ridge overhanging the valley of the Camlad began.
Building went on rapidly; the official rolls record the stages and
costs, and the fact that the work is constantly referred to as 'New
Montgomery' does suggest that Earl Roger's original strongpoint
was on a different site.

This was at a period when Hubert de Burgh, the king's justiciar,
was at the height of his powers, and certainly had an appetite for
castles, lands and influence, so that Llewelyn the Great, then prince
of Gwynedd and married to King Henry's half-sister Joan, had good
reason to keep a watchful eye on his borders, and cause to look on
in some concern when in 1228 the king bestowed the castle and
lordship of Montgomery upon the justiciar. His suspicions were
soon justified when Hubert began the clearing and felling of the
forest land south-west of the castle, opening the approach to the
wholly Welsh commote of Kerry. The Welsh of the district gathered in alarm to watch developments. Llewelyn trusted in a peaceable settlement, and his most influential envoy, his wife the Princess
Joan, met her half-brother at Shrewsbury to arrange a truce, and
there was a polite pause during which courteous letters passed
between king and prince. But not for long. The leading Marchers
gathered at Montgomery – Clares, de Breoses, Cliffords and all – at
a royal summons most probably urged upon the king by de Burgh,
the feudal host advanced into Welsh Kerry, and Hubert began to
build a new castle there as a base for further intrusion.

This was a direct challenge to Llewelyn, and he took it up
cheerfully, blessed with the backing of every soul in the commote,
excellent knowledge of a very complex and difficult country, and
armed with a legitimate grievance. The campaign ended,
inevitably, in an ignominious retreat into England for the royal
forces, and the abandonment of all plans for a conquest of Kerry.
William de Breose, the lord of Builth, was captured, and spent
some time in captivity in Llewelyn's *Ilys* until the settlement. The
ransom he paid for his release was £2,000, the same sum as the

Montgomery Castle.

indemnity Llewelyn paid to recompense the royal exchequer for the total demolition of Hubert's half-built castle. The one sum cancelled out the other, no doubt by design.

This humiliation, like any such visited upon Henry III, was bound to be avenged upon a scapegoat of some sort, and here there was a ready one to hand in Hubert de Burgh. Again, in some sort the king had been trapped into a situation where he had to back down ignominiously, and that was unforgivable. The rout of Kerry probably played a part in the justiciar's coming disgrace and persecution.

There was yet another end to the campaign, even more tragic. William de Breose, prisoner for some months at Llewelyn's court, was a young man of about twenty-seven, most likely very attractive. The Princess Joan was a mature woman turned forty, with a husband who, however deeply loved and loyally served, was as often absent as present. There is every reason to suppose that what resulted was a genuine and serious passion for both of them. For there is no other shadow of a disloyalty in Joan's entire married life; and the man felt strongly enough to risk continuing the liaison on a later visit, when he was Llewelyn's guest.

De Breose paid with his life when Llewelyn discovered the affair. He hanged the lover, and kept Joan in close confinement for a year. There were no repercussions. England accepted the justice of the sentence, and made no move to avenge the death. A year later Llewelyn and Joan were reconciled, and she became, as before, his most trusted ambassador and best councillor. They were exceptional people, both. It was William de Breose's misfortune that he fell into waters and destinies so far out of his depth.

It was in the early summer of 1231 that prince and princess were reconciled, at a time when Llewelyn was about to take the field again in defence of his realm and his son's inheritance. De Burgh had sent out a raiding party, or his castellan had, into Welsh territory, and taken a number of prisoners. The justiciar, visiting his castle, ordered that all the captives should be beheaded. It was the last straw in a series of offences, and Llewelyn felt it time to take action. At such a crisis he chose to leave his home affairs in the pair of hands he most trusted, even now. He brought Joan out of her retirement to be his best lieutenant as she always had.

'Yes, speak of him,' said Llewelyn. 'It's meet we should. It's time we should.'

'He was blown in the storm as I was, however the thing began. Your rival he never was. You never had a rival.' The beautiful voice bled words in short, hard sighs into his arm. 'When he came he was weak and in pain. And so young! He needed all those things in me for which you had no use, pity, indulgence, even forgiveness. By his youth he showed me how late it was, and by his admiration that it was not yet too late. He made me know that I was growing old, and that everything he was was slipping out of my hands. And I closed my hands and grasped it while I could. And then I could not loose.' . . .

'You it never touched,' she said. 'Your place it never threatened. The world would not see it so, but I tell you, this is truth. And yet it all but shattered your life and mine and all our work, and killed an unfortunate, rash young man no worse than the most of men, and hardly deserving of death. Night and day, I never can forget him.'

'You need not,' said Llewelyn, 'as I have not forgotten him. Wherever we go, he will go with us, that I know. But he will not go always between us.'

THE GREEN BRANCH

Rhyd Chwima, the Ford of Montgomery

Down the blanched and rustling meadows Llewelyn rode, to the spit of sand and turf that ran out into the river, and all we after him. Into the shallow water he splashed, and the silver danced at his horse's heels. When he rode up the greensward on the further shore, towards where King Henry sat before the pavilion on a gilded throne, royal esquires came to take his bridle, and all we who served him dismounted with him and lined the shore. The king's knights kneeled to take off his spurs and ungird the swordbelt from his loins. He wore no mail and no gauntlets, and his head was uncovered, and thus he walked alone up the slope of green turf, his sombre brown made resplendent with scarlet and gold, and kneeled upon the gilded footstool at the king's feet, lifting to him his joined hands and his fierce and joyful face.

King Henry sat in shade, just at the rim of the pavilion's canopy, for the brightness of the sun somewhat troubled his eyes. But Llewelyn kneeled in sunlight, and when he raised his head the sunbeams blazed upon him, and touched his sunburned face into minted gold, and the king paled and dwindled into a spectre beside him, like a candle in the noonday.

In a loud, clear voice Llewelyn rehearsed the oath of fealty, saving his own sovereign right within Wales, while the king's thin white hands, a little knotted with increasing age, enclosed his own. And thus he became vassal to King Henry and magnate of England, and also acknowledged prince of Wales, at sworn peace with his neighbour. And as he owed allegiance to the king, so did the king owe the loyal support and protection of his overlordship to Llewelyn, with right and justice in return for his feudal due.

THE DRAGON AT NOONDAY

This was the glittering scene that took place once in this now shadowed, mysterious and melancholy spot. The ford of Montgomery, Rhyd Chwima, Rhydwhyman now on the map, had been for generations one of the traditional meeting-places on the border, perhaps the most important one, where Welsh and English authorities came together to deal with complaints upon either

side, make agreements, and sort out differences in times of peace between the two countries. And here, on the twenty-seventh day of September, in the year 1267, this most vital meeting of king and prince took place, the formal ratification of the Treaty of Montgomery, Llewelyn's triumph, and the apotheosis of his life-long ambitions for Wales.

It was two years since he had achieved the Treaty of Pipton, in King Henry's name but through the medium of Simon de Montfort, then briefly and precariously master of England. Now he had wrested, from a king freed but beset by the last throes of the Barons' War, virtually every concession Simon had promised in the royal name. The papal legate, Cardinal Ottobuono Fieschi, played an honourable part as intermediary, and won a few years of peace for a Wales which now was very close to becoming a sovereign nation state.

Only after the death of a king mellowing into amiability and patience in his later years, and the accession of a returned Crusader, a young, energetic, acquisitive giant at the height of his powers, did the inevitable collision begin.

Acton Burnell

In the refectory of Shrewsbury Abbey . . . Edward the king caused his sometime darling to be brought to trial of high treason, murder and sundry other grave charges, before the lords of Parliament assembled, and judges duly appointed by the king himself, presiding in his own cause, though in absence. They say he spent those days as guest of his chancellor, who had a princely mansion not far from the town. Certain it is that Edward never confronted David after his capture, never once encountered him eye to eye. He hung aloof at Acton Burnell, devouring his own gall and savouring the messages that brought him degree after degree of triumph over his enemy.

Yet what monarch who feels himself triumphant need exact what he exacted? I judge rather that he felt himself eternally bested, by what infernal arts only Llewelyn and David knew. How else to account for his malignant venom?

AFTERGLOW AND NIGHTFALL

LEFT

Ford across the River Severn, Montgomery

Acton Burnell Castle, built about 1284 by Robert Burnell who became Lord Chancellor and Bishop of Bath and Wells.

The princely mansion to which King Edward repaired with his chancellor Robert Burnell, during the parliament called at Shrewsbury in 1283 to witness the condemnation and execution of Prince David of Wales cannot have been the red sandstone tower house standing now in majestic ruin, but a previous family residence and great hall, to which the two huge remaining gable-ends in the grounds may have belonged. Robert Burnell's licence to crenellate was issued to him the following year, together with permission to take timber from the royal forest for his building plans.

It has often been supposed that the parliament itself met at Acton Burnell, and the gables are sometimes referred to as the Parliament Barn, but it is far more likely that trial and penalty would not be withdrawn from the town, where the abbey was by far the most convenient place to meet, and the most official and commodious. Crowds of witnesses would be desirable to look on at Edward's vengeance. It was not enough that the extreme penalty should be public. Justice had to be seen to be done.

It is a wonderful place now, with that huge pile, solitary, silent except for birds, even though there are houses and a church close by. All that arresting, arrogant red bathed and swathed all round and bedded in the greenest of greens, for it stands in a grassy, shallow bowl not far from marsh. In the driest of weather, the turf of Acton Burnell remains viridian, to set off the blood-red ruin the chancellor left behind.

The Castles of Welshpool: Powis

On the last day of November, in a cloudy and melancholy afternoon light, we five rode into the town of Pool, and down to the river meadows, where the castle was raised. We bore no arms, and went unattended, in token of the openness and honesty of our intent, and at the castle gates asked audience of Griffith in the name of the prince of Wales, his overlord, on matters of state. Peaceable as our aspect was, it aroused a great deal of fluttering within, until Griffith sent word in haste to admit us at once, and himself came hurrying out in his furred gown to meet us on the steps of his great hall. His heavy-featured face bore a fixed and somewhat ungainly smile, with little true welcome in it, but a great effort at appearing welcoming. He bore himself as though nothing had happened since April, when he had confessed to disloyalty, and resigned himself to the loss of some part of his lands, and the enforced absence of his eldest son. Having cleared that account in full, his manner seemed to say, there can be nothing in this visit now to trouble my conscience, and nothing to fear. But his eyes looked sidelong, and were not quite easy.

THE HOUNDS OF SUNSET

This was the visit of Llewelyn's envoys to his vassal Griffith ap Gwenwynwyn of Powys in 1274, after David's last and worst betrayal, which had involved plotting the murder of the prince, and the installation of David in his place, through an armed conspiracy with Griffith and his family. The plot was frustrated by appalling weather, but eventually the truth leaked out. Llewelyn, uncertain whether Griffith himself had been involved, and willing to restrain his natural anger in order to keep Wales together, sent in good faith to try to bring about a reasonable reconciliation. His

envoys were thrown into the dungeons, and Griffith and all his family fled into Shrewsbury, where David had already taken refuge. King Edward, recognizing useful weapons when they were offered to his hand, ordered his sheriff to give them shelter and every assistance in their instant campaign of malice in arms against the prince from the safety of Shrewsbury. In return Llewelyn took and slighted the castle of Pool, released his men, and possessed himself of the entire lands of his traitorous vassal.

There is something of a puzzle to work out the exact location and number of the castles connected with Welshpool. There was certainly an old Welsh castle of Trallwng, the name also applied to the town of Welshpool. This castle, Sir John Lloyd tells us in his *History of Wales from the Earliest Times to the Edwardian Conquest*, was 'known to the English as Pool'. Llewelyn the Great of Gwynedd also had a certain Castell Coch somewhere in the neighbourhood, as distinct from Griffith ap Gwenwynwyn's castle of Pool. The

LEFT AND ABOVE

The terrace of Powis Castle, nearly 200 metres long, overlooks the lower gardens. It was built in the eighteenth century by the Earl of Rochford.

The abbey of Strata Marcella once stood on these banks of the River Severn near Welshpool, but now the river meadows are used for grazing.

Ordnance Survey map has two motte and bailey sites marked, one by the river close to the town, one further along the ridge where Powis Castle now stands. It seems reasonable to suppose that Griffith's stronghold lay close beside the town, while Llewelyn's Castell Coch occupied approximately the site of the present Powis Castle, a fine defensible position with commanding views.

Strata Marcella

On these green meadows by the Severn near Welshpool, with the Breiddens rising in the distance, once stood the Cistercian abbey of Strata Marcella, founded in 1170 from Whitland. The land was given by Owain Cyfeiliog, a prince of Powys and a noted poet. The commote of Ystrad Marchell gave the house its Latin name of Strata Marcella, and this abbey in turn was the mother of Valle Crucis. The daughter still stands, impressive and dignified; almost every trace of the mother house is gone.

A great scandal overshadowed the career of the first abbot, according to Gerald of Wales. Abbot Enoch was a very earnest and diligent man, who set out to found a house for Cistercian nuns at Llansantffraid, and succumbed to temptation when he fell in love with one of the nuns, a beautiful woman from a good family. They took the plunge and eloped together, setting off a scandal that rocked the order in Wales. Eventually Enoch repented, or at any rate returned to his abbey and resumed the claustral life, but the proposed nunnery never came into valid being, and we do not learn what happened to the lady.

Strata Marcella survived the shame, and played an illustrious part in the monastic history of Wales. Time, neglect and solitude have finally obliterated its name and the last mention of it even from Ordnance Survey maps.

OVERLEAF

A few stones atop a hill near Valle Crucis Abbey are all that remain of Castell Dinas Bran, an eighth-century castle.

Shrewsbury and Glendower Country

North of Shrewsbury, a river town if ever there was, seat of quarrels and conferences in equal measure during the high period of the marcher baronies, the Severn turns east and south from its guardianship of the borders, and hands over precedence to the River Dee. Beyond the north Shropshire strongholds of Whittington and Oswestry, and the cadet Mortimer holding of Chirk, begins the beautiful Vale of Llangollen, with the great hog's back and gnarled walls of Dinas Bran looming over it. Just a few miles upstream from Llangollen itself lies Glyndyfrdwy, the ancestral home of the family of Owen Glendower. The name the English use for the last great native prince of Wales is derived from the place of his birth. Owen held from the English Crown lands his ancestors had ruled as princes, and his rebellion, fuelled by a land-feud with Lord Grey of Ruthin, in which he felt, probably rightly, that no Welshman would ever win the verdict against an English baron, held England at bay for fifteen years, from 1400 to 1415, when he vanished from history, like the wizard he was esteemed by many. He was never taken; as far as records can testify, he never died. He survived the defeat of his alliance with Mortimer and the Percys, which brought about Hotspur's death at the battle of Shrewsbury, and the death of his son-in-law Edmund Mortimer at the siege of Harlech in 1409. On Saint Matthew's Day in 1415 he went into hiding, and nothing more is ever recorded of him. Like Merlin, when his prime was past and his powers spent he withdrew untamed and intact into a cloud of legend.

Across the Dee, only a mile or so from Llangollen, lies the beautiful ruin of Valle Crucis Abbey, daughter-house of Strata Marcella, the lost lady of the Severn meadows near Welshpool; and only a step beyond, and centuries older still, stands the now headless cross of Elisedd, or Eliseg, which gave its name to the valley and the monastery.

The west door into the ruined nave of Valle Crucis Abbey.

The Wrekin

Before him, beyond the level of fields, rose the wooded hogback of the
Wrekin, and soon the river reappeared at some distance on his left, to
wind nearer as he proceeded, until it was close beside the highway, a
gentle, innocent stream between flat, grassy banks, incapable of
menace to all appearances, though the local people knew better than
to trust it.

THE HERETIC'S APPRENTICE

Abrupt and volcanic, springing solitary out of the plain, the earthworks of Heaven Gate and Hell Gate on this little mountain were the defences of the British tribe of the Cornovii, before they came to amicable terms with the Romans, and came down into the plain to populate the settlement and town of Uriconium.

Before the Romans came to nearby Wroxeter (Uriconium) the Cornovii tribe had a fort on top of Wrekin Hill.

Atcham Church by the River Severn

A red sandstone church at Atcham by the River Severn, the only church dedicated to St Eata. It has some Norman features.

There were cattle in the pastures here, and waterfowl among the fringes of reeds. And soon he could see the square, squat tower of the parish church of Saint Eata beyond the curve of the Severn, and the low roofs of the village clustered close to it. There was a wooden bridge somewhat to the left, but Cadfael made straight for the church and the priest's house beside it. Here the river spread out into a maze of green and golden shallows, and at this summer level could easily be forded. Cadfael tucked up his habit and splashed through, shaking the little rafts of water crowfoot until the whole languid surface quivered.

THE HERETIC'S APPRENTICE

Here is a scene which has not changed very greatly since the twelfth century; though the red sandstone church has been embellished and restored from time to time; the sacred site, the foundation and the unique dedication were all here in 1075, when Shropshire's great medieval historian, Orderic Vitalis, was baptized here, and given the name of the officiating priest. The boy's father was one of Earl Roger de Montgomery's chaplains, and had come over from Normandy with him, but here in Shropshire, where clerical marriage was still quite legal, Odelerius had married an Englishwoman, and brought into the world the greatest chronicler of his age. There is no other church known to be dedicated to St Eata, who was one of the companions of St Aidan.

Shrewsbury

As a border town in command of a crossing of the Severn, and itself well protected by a great loop of the river, and the erection of a castle commanding the only dryshod approach, Shrewsbury naturally played a prominent part in the history of the March of Wales. Like the north Shropshire town of Oswestry, it was virtually as much Welsh as English, and at times incorporated into Wales. An old foundation, with four established parish churches

Looking south from the old
Shrewsbury Infirmary to the English
Bridge built over the River Severn in
the eighteenth century.

within its comparatively constricted bounds, even before the abbey
was founded, and sharing the control of the middle March with
Oswestry to the north and Montgomery to the south in the earliest
years of the Norman invasion, it was clearly a suitable region for a
very strong earldom, only second in privileges to that of Chester.
The Montgomery earls built the castle and developed the small
wooden church outside the loop of the river into the Benedictine
abbey. They held the earldom until 1102, when Robert of
Bellême, many years a thorn in the flesh of the Crown, was finally
arraigned by Henry I and fled to Normandy to continue making
trouble, and the fortress of Shrewsbury was administered by
Crown officials. In the anarchy of Stephen's reign it suffered siege
and capture by the king's forces, its castellan, FitzAlan, having
made a stand for the empress, but FitzAlan regained his status after
the final settlement, when Henry II assumed the crown.

When a full-scale attack on Wales was contemplated, involving
the muster of the feudal host and the movement of large numbers
of men and supplies, Shrewsbury was usually one of the gathering

places from which it was launched. Twice at least the host moved in from here, only to be defeated ignominiously by Welsh topography and Welsh weather. In 1165 Henry II gathered the feudal host here, plus contingents from his overseas holdings and mercenaries from Flanders. A fleet was hired from the Danish kingdom of Dublin, as so often in history by kings or aggrieved barons both Welsh and English, to support by sea. Crossing the Berwyns in wild weather, bogged down by numbers and running short of supplies, Henry withdrew his bedraggled forces with nothing gained.

Again, in 1402, at the beginning of autumn, Henry IV planned a threefold assault on Owen Glendower, to end his menace once and for all; from Chester, Shrewsbury and Hereford, three prongs would advance into Wales and hunt him out of all his coverts. Prince Hal commanded the Chester contingent, held them under tight control, taking no unnecessary risks, covered the northern ground he was sent to cover, and never encountered any Welsh force to fight. They melted away, and he did not follow them into fastnesses where they would be at an advantage. He brought his army back unbruised but ineffective. The Hereford force, thought to have been under the Earl of Stafford, hunted Glendower in the south without great loss to themselves, but never caught up with him. The king went in from Shrewsbury, through a well-provisioned advance base at Welshpool, into the Cambrian mountains, and into appalling storms that swelled all the rivers and brooks, drowned all the upland bogs, rendered hillsides treacherous, and finally, where the royal army was encamped in tents, lightning struck the king's piled armour, beside which the royal lance was fixed upright, fused the plate-armour into a tangle of metal, and reduced the king's standard to a charred rag. Henry retreated into Shrewsbury in black humiliation.

Shrewsbury has also been the setting for vital conferences and the seat of parliaments, the most notable being Edward I's parliament of 1283, convened expressly to stage the public show-trial of Prince David of Wales, and his execution, after Edward's final annexation of the whole of that country.

During the reign of King John the perpetual problems of border people were summed up in the person of one woman, the king's daughter Joan, married to Llewelyn the Great of Wales. Eternally engaged in holding together things hostility threatened to break

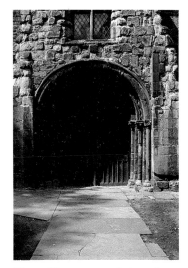

The twelfth-century south door of St Mary's church, Shrewsbury.

apart, Joan was perhaps the most indomitable maker and sustainer of truce in the history of the March. Time after time she met her father, and later Henry III, her half-brother, at Shrewsbury to smooth out arguments between the two, and to try to fend off warfare. On 6 December 1232, in St Mary's church, she led a delegation from her husband at a conference met to consider how best to sort out all disputes from either side of the border. King Henry had asked for papal intervention, and the Pope's legates were present. Joan and her son David, with their Welsh legal men and officials, set out the tale of Llewelyn's complaints, the Marcher barons set out theirs. Truce was continued, and an independent commission set up with representatives from both lands, to adjudicate on all future disputes. At about this same time St Mary's was acquiring, in a bout of new building, the added aisles, and the round-arched, slender-piered arcading that divides them off from the nave, with their splendid stiff-leaf capitals.

St Mary's church is the oldest ecclesiastical foundation in Shrewsbury, founded *c.* 965 by King Edgar. The present church was started *c.* 1140 and there are considerable remains from that period.

The church at Battlefield, built by Henry IV in memory of the fallen in the Battle of Shrewsbury, 1403.

Battlefield

On Sunday there were services of thanksgiving in all the churches of Shrewsbury, the bells pealed, and the king heard Mass after Mass to his comfort and consolation. The rest of the day was given to the pious duty of burying the dead, of whom by now there were some four thousand, besides those of birth and coat-armour whose kin had already conveyed them to the grave. Citizens, peasants and soldiers were all recruited to the sacred labour, and the summer being so high, and time so short for so many obsequies, there was no alternative but to make one great mass grave upon the battlefield, and there lay all the slain of both parties together, to wait for judgement day.

So they did. And so they wait still.

A Bloody Field by Shrewsbury

This was the aftermath of the battle of Shrewsbury, fought on 21 July 1403. It was a Saturday. The Percys had planned on possessing Shrewsbury and joining forces on the Monday with their allies from Wales, but Henry IV had moved with quite uncharacteristic speed and entered Shrewsbury before they could reach it, and forced the battle two days before the Welsh contingent under Mortimer and Glendower could arrive.

The church of Battlefield was built over the mass grave.

Moreton Corbet church, from the nave looking into the south chapel (or Squire's pew) which was built in 1778 and contains memorials to the Corbet family.

Moreton Corbet

The first Corbet came over with the Conqueror, bringing with him his second and fourth sons, Roger and Robert FitzCorbet, having left behind in Normandy the first and third sons, Hugh and Renaud. They were an energetic and durable line, on both sides of the sea. Renaud and his two sons were in Palestine in the First Crusade, and succeeding generations in the Norman line continued the tradition in later Crusades. Branches of the family spread into Flanders and into Spain. In England, Roger FitzCorbet was given the lordship of Alretone in Shropshire, by Earl Roger de Montgomery, and built there a castle to which he gave the name of Caus, after the Pays de Caux in Normandy, from which his forebears came. He was an able lieutenant to the earl in protecting and expanding the Shropshire border into Wales. The original Caus

RIGHT

A view of the twelfth-century church and castle at Moreton Corbet through a door opening in the ruined sixteenth-century mansion.

castle is now a green, wooded mound; midway between Shrewsbury and Welshpool, it commanded the valley of the Rea Brook, and saw very frequent action in the border raids. But other scions of the vigorous clan held other properties, and the name is still widespread in the county. All the Shropshire Corbets, according to John Corbet Anderson, author of the 1864 *Shropshire: Its Early History and Antiquities*, are descended from the Domesday baron, Roger FitzCorbet.

Moreton Corbet, near Shawbury, is an astonishing group of buildings: a very fine church with features from every period, from the Norman chancel, through Tudor, Elizabethan and Jacobean tomb monuments, to a great deal of late eighteenth-century embellishments; the ruins of a Norman castle from about 1200, with a gatehouse; and the magnificent, towering shell of an Elizabethan mansion, never finished, and damaged by warfare and fire in the Civil War.

Whittington Castle

Whittington was a royal manor under Edward the Confessor, and when Roger de Montgomery was made Earl of Shrewsbury by the Conqueror, and allotted some of the properties that fell to him to other of his supporters, he kept Whittington in his own hands. Later it came into the possession of the FitzWarrens, and in 1223 the castle was captured from them and held for a while by Llewelyn the Great, Prince of Gwynedd.

In the war of the baronage against Henry III, Simon de Montfort, in the name of the reformed government which had the captive king in its hold, met Llewelyn ap Griffith and made a treaty with him at Pipton; by the terms of this agreement Llewelyn was granted three Marcher castles, Hawarden in the north, Whittington in the centre, and Painscastle in the south, for the better protection of his own gains, and in return for his support in Simon's current difficulties. Llewelyn was prepared to pay an indemnity of 30,000 marks for the grant of the castles, to be rendered in ten annual instalments, and also pledged in return his peace and fealty towards the king, so long as the government adhered to the present reforms.

The gatehouse of Whittington Castle built by Fulke FitzWarine in the reign of Henry III as an improvement to the old castle.

After the death and defeat of the Montfort cause and its champion, in the final settlement Llewelyn achieved all that had been promised him at Pipton, and at the Peace of Montgomery the amount of the indemnity became 25,000 marks instead of 30,000. It is noteworthy that until mutual suspicion made the rift between Edward and Llewelyn unbridgeable, the instalments were paid promptly and in full.

Chirk Castle

Before the Edwardian conquest the commote of Chirk belonged to the lands of Griffith ap Madog, one of the princes of Powys, who was the builder of the castle at Dinas Bran, but after his death his son, being a minor, came into the guardianship of the Crown, and both he and his lands were placed in the care of the Justice of North Wales in the new dispensation, who happened to be Roger Mortimer. Building was in progress here, at the king's instigation, as early as 1294, though this may have been merely a case of strengthening a former fortress on the site, for the present impressive stronghold, completed by the Mortimers, was finished in 1310.

Though there had been the usual to-and-fro of Anglo–Welsh raiding along the March in these parts as elsewhere, Chirk had not played a very involved and turbulent part in the inter-racial struggle of the former two centuries, and after the pacification of Wales it survived intact to enjoy a peaceful life until the Civil War. Even so, the tale of its successive owners reads like a list of the great Marcher families. It passed from the Mortimers to the FitzAlans, by marriage to a Mowbray, Earl of Norfolk, to a lord of Abergavenny, and then to Sir John Stanley during the Wars of the Roses. Eventually, in 1595, it came into possession of the Myddelton family.

In the Civil War it was held for Parliament by Sir Thomas Myddelton, but was seized by the Royalists during his absence in the service of Cromwell. Somewhat later a disillusioned Sir Thomas changed his mind about Cromwell, and declared for Charles II, and his family were able to establish a long tenure of Chirk from the Restoration to the present day.

The River Dee at Glyndyfrdwy

'Who was that?' Hotspur demanded with raised brows. 'The fellow who went out in a fury?'

'Some Welsh kern with a grievance against Lord Grey. There's a plot of ground in dispute between them, somewhere in Glyndyfrdwy. The king would not see him.'

'Welsh?' the prince echoed, and jerked his chin over his shoulder to stare after the vanished appellant.

'It seems we shall have interesting neighbours in Chester,' Hotspur remarked, and his smile was still a little astonished, and more than a little thoughtful. 'Take good note of the face, Hal, for if he keeps his present mind we may well be seeing more of it. How is he called, this Welsh kern with a grievance?'

RIGHT

Dating from *c.* 1310 Chirk was one of the strongest castles in the Welsh Marches.

Owen Glendower took his English name from the Glyndyfrdwy valley on the River Dee.

'Oh, he's more than that, I grant you. He's a gentleman of coat-armour, and married to Sir David Hanmer's daughter, his master in the Inns,' said Sir Thomas Rempston the steward. 'They call him Owen of Glendower.'

A BLOODY FIELD BY SHREWSBURY

In Henry IV's dismissal of all claims at law against Lord Grey of Ruthin, whose tight hold on his Welsh neighbours was valuable to the Crown, lay the seed of the Glendower rebellion. It was from this beautiful stretch of the Dee valley that Owen took his usual English name, deriving Glendower from Glyndyfrdwy, for here was his native place and his heritage.

The hostility between Owen and Grey continued in arms for some years, and in April of 1402 Owen captured his enemy and held him to ransom. It was King Henry's haste to recover Grey and flat refusal to do as much for Edmund Mortimer, also a prisoner in Wales, that finally alienated Hotspur, caused Mortimer to join forces with his princely Welsh captor, and precipitated Crown and country into the slaughter of the battle of Shrewsbury.

The Pillar of Elisedd (or Eliseg), from
which Valle Crucis gets its name (The
Valley of the Cross).

The Pillar of Elisedd

The name is more usually found as 'Eliseg', but Sir John Lloyd
considers that it should more probably be read as Elisedd, the old
form of Elis or Elise. It stands on a small mound on the right side
of the road climbing up from Valle Crucis. Long ago it lost the
crowning cross that gave the name to the valley and the monastery,
and the inscription on the pillar is eroded beyond reading now. But
it was erected in glorification of the royal line of Powys, and in
particular of this prince, Elisedd, who ruled in the middle of the
eighth century. His great-grandson set up the stone in his ances-
tor's honour.

Shropshire's two clerical historians, Owen and Blakeway, com-
piling their *History of Shrewsbury* early in the nineteenth century,
recorded that Robert Vaughan, a well-known antiquary, took a
copy of the inscription as it then was, in 1662. They give a copy of
the original broken lines of Latin, and translate them thus:

Concenn was the son of Cattell, Cattell
the son of Brohcmail, Brohcmail the son
of Eliseg, Eliseg the son of Guoillauc.

Concenn therefore the great-grandson of Eliseg
built this stone to his great-grandfather
Eliseg + This is the Eliseg who recovered
his inheritance of Povosia after the death
of Cattell by force out of the power of the Angles
by his sword . . . . fire
. . . . . restored the inscription . . . .
                    blessing upon
Eliseg + This is Concenn

                    . . . .
            his kingdom of Povosia
                    . . . . which
                    . . . . death

. . . .
. . . . the monarchy
. . . . Maximus of Britain
Pascentius . . . .
. . . . son of Guarthi
whom Germanus blessed, whom
bore to him S.eira daughter of Maximus
the king who slew the king of the Romans
+ Conmarch engraved this
inscription at the request of his king
Concenn + May the blessing of the lord be upon Concenn
and . . . . . on his whole family
and on the whole region of Povois
for . . . .

This Maximus, here dual-natured between legend and history, was the Spanish soldier in Roman service who at the end of the fourth century gained the support of the legions in Britain and induced them to elect him emperor, and crossing with his troops into Gaul, for some years ruled Gaul, Britain and Spain, according to history not at all badly or tyrannically, but lost his gains and his life in attempting the conquest of Italy itself, and was defeated by Theodosius. The Welsh, says Sir John Lloyd, knew him as Macsen

Wledig. It is his story that Kipling tells in the epic Roman section of *Puck of Pook's Hill*.

Valle Crucis

The Cistercian abbey of Valle Crucis was founded in 1201 by Madoc ap Griffith Maelor, Prince of Powys, colonized as a daughter-house of the abbey of Strata Marcella, near Welshpool. Monks and lay brothers from the mother-house came to settle in the beautiful valley where stood the celebratory pillar of a former prince of Powys, Elise, and took the name of their monastery from the cross which topped the record of his achievements. Like most Cistercian sites, the spot is solitary and quiet, and its history seems to have been tranquil and uneventful.

Dinas Bran

We closed in from three sides upon Dinas Bran, high on its great grassy ridge above the river valley. We from the north, approaching over the hills, had the best ground for attack, and came as the greatest shock to a garrison that thought us still busy with Rhuddlan and Flint. Moreover, I would not say the watch they kept was very competent, or we should not have got within striking distance of the main gatehouse before they gave the alarm. Speed, which had been our greatest asset in reaching them so soon, was also our strongest weapon in attack. They never had time to get the bars into their sockets before we stove in the doors and were among them, and put our first parties up onto the walls to dispose of their archers, not only to have a commanding ring round the mêlée in the castle ward, but also to prevent them from shooting down upon our friends from Cynllaith as they stormed up the hill to join us. After that it was no great feat of arms, and cost us but a few men wounded, to get possession of the whole castle with most of the garrison, though Lestrange himself, with a small, well-mounted party got out by a postern gate when he saw the castle was lost, and made clean away before we knew he was loose. But Dinas Bran was ours to garrison afresh for Wales, and the Welsh of those parts were eager and ready to man it in the prince's name.

Thus we held, within a few days, a strong line of castles running south-

east from the sea almost to Oswestry, and guarding the whole of the northern March fronting Chester: from the north Denbigh, Ruthin and Dinas Bran, with Rhuddlan itself still in English hands but isolated at the northern extreme of the line, and Hope a somewhat vulnerable but as yet useful outpost, much nearer to Chester.

AFTERGLOW AND NIGHTFALL

This was the Welsh situation in the spring of 1282.

OVERLEAF

Llyn Brenig, in the wild landscape of
the hills above Ruthin and Denbigh.

The Last Bastion: Llewelyn's Gwynedd

Gwynedd, the north-western fortress of the mountains of Snowdonia, was always the heart and foundation of Wales, the keep of the nation's castle; but its approaches from England were by comparison soft and vulnerable. It only remained for an English king, more ambitious, more able and more ruthless than any of his predecessors, to achieve a sufficient force by land and by sea, equipped better than ever before with siege-engines, the means of transport and efficient control of the commissariat, and Wales could be conquered. There is no castle keep that cannot be starved out, once the outer and inner baileys are taken. And that is what happened to Snowdonia in the final war of 1282. The roads had been opened beforehand by armies of foresters and engineers. The ships had been massed in the Cinque Ports and brought round to Anglesey and the estuary of the Dee, then navigable. Retreat into the mountains was no longer a solution, for there was force enough deployed to pen an army there, and time and winter no longer presented any respite.

So in the last campaign the border castles, though in the first assault they might fall to the impetuous Welsh, just as inevitably were picked off again into English hands as soon as Edward's war machine got into ponderous motion. Its slowness no longer mattered. It could maintain and accelerate its advance, once launched. Hope and Denbigh, in danger of being outflanked, were abandoned; Hawarden, Ruthin, Dinas Bran, Flint, Rhuddlan, all those taken, all those cut off and surrounded, fell back into English possession. Even the citadel of Snowdon was at last surrounded, until Edward could gradually compress it bailey by bailey, and starve out its defenders. The broad, accessible roads in from Chester had served their purpose. The castle fell.

LEFT

Looking south from the ramparts of
Denbigh Castle to the Vale of Clwyd.

Caergwrle: The Castle of Hope

*T*hus we accompanied the royal army almost to Chester, where they arrived about the tenth day of June, and then we drew off and left them, rejoining David in Hope. He had had fighting, too, for Reginald de Grey had sent out a strong company under one of his bannerets to probe up the valley of the Dee and establish a forward post some miles south of the city, and though the Welsh had contested the attempt and cost them heavy losses, Grey had reinforced the camp, and David had not been able to dislodge him.

'He is already thinking he can cut me off here,' he said, 'and so he might, if I had any intention of staying here to fall into his hands. Hope has served its purpose. In a few days I think we must give it to him – what's left of it!'

Three days we spent dismantling the defences, breaching the walls, undermining the towers, and the broken masonry and rubble we emptied into the two castle wells until they were filled up and useless. What David did to his well-loved fortress cost the English two months' delay, and a great sum to repair. When it was done, and the whole site desolate, we drew off into the hills to westward.

AFTERGLOW AND NIGHTFALL

Always the most vulnerable, and the first to have to be surrendered, Hope fell into English hands early in the final war. After victory, in his settlement of 1283, Edward gave the Castle of Hope to his queen, Eleanor of Castille.

Ruthin Castle

Time was then the most precious and effective ally we had, to waste it on winning such a castle as Rhuddlan would have lost us weeks, if not months, that we could not afford. There were other strongholds more vulnerable, and of greater use to us, and Llewelyn had already marked them down.

Hope Castle was one of the many castles built by Henry I in his conquest of Wales.

'Ruthin is not so firmly held, and they never look to see us there, the coast roads being their best approach and our greatest weakness. Now the men of Maelor are up, we have allies there to help us. We should do well to move up the Clwyd, and send ahead to them to meet us, you at Ruthin, me at Dinas Bran. If we move fast enough we may get both, and have a line of castles down the March.'

'Lestrange has newly garrisoned Dinas Bran,' said David.

'So much the better, he'll be over confident.'

AFTERGLOW AND NIGHTFALL

Ruthin was the second castle to fall to the Welsh in the war of 1282. At first the sheer unexpectedness of the rising brought successes, but from the first it was inevitable that once the more ponderous but far more deadly English war-machine got into motion, this first fortune must reverse.

Ruthin played a part later in the time of Glendower's campaigns, for Lord Grey of Ruthin was the baron who had a long-standing legal dispute with the Welsh prince, and it was Owen's capture of Grey, and Henry IV's haste to ransom him while refusing to do as much for Mortimer, that led to the breach with the Percys, and the battle of Shrewsbury.

Denbigh Castle

Denbigh being the best base from which to control and guard all that long eastern March, Llewelyn made it his headquarters until David's party should again come north, and though we were often out patrolling the line of fortresses, and sometimes withdrew to Conway and Aber and the western cantrefs to deploy the incoming levies as they mustered, it was always to Denbigh we returned. Such fighting as we had was limited to testing raids along the border. It seemed that all the barons of the March were putting their followings on a fighting footing, but not yet making any move to attack, rather merely holding their defences. We heard, but not with certainty, that a royal muster was expected in May at Worcester, but had heard no word of the usual summons going out for the assembly of the feudal host.

AFTERGLOW AND NIGHTFALL

At this time Denbigh and Hope were in David's possession lawfully, under the recent treaty, and while Hope was perilously exposed in the east, Denbigh was held for some time as the base of operations in the north. A gathering of all the princes of Wales was held here early in the campaign, to co-ordinate the effort in every field; for once, Wales was united, though in a society still obstinately tribal such unity was liable to disintegrate under pressure. However, they held Denbigh until Edward had his entire force organized and in action, and gradually David's castle, like Hope before it, was in danger of being outflanked and trapped. Then David withdrew his garrison, leaving a castellan to surrender Denbigh on the best terms he could get, without provoking Edward into any vengeance against the skeleton force left to man it.

The lordship was conferred by Edward on the Earl of Lincoln; but even afterwards there were eruptions of resentment among the Welsh of Denbigh, ending with the last brief blaze of rebellion in 1295.

Looking northwards over Denbigh from the castle gates. The foreground tower is all that remains of the fourteenth-century garrison chapel.

Hawarden Castle

Tudor ab Ednyfed, the high steward of Wales, had a manor in Tegaingl. And that being one of the cantrefs of the Middle Country retained by King Edward in his own hands, Tudor now held his lands there of the king, and had all the vexations common to all those in that situation, wholly loyal to the prince, but owing formal fealty also to Edward for one manor. Such were the complications that he was forced to pay frequent visits to his tenants there, and at this time he rode thence to join us for Easter.

This keep is all that remains of the original Hawarden Castle built in the thirteenth century.

He was not expected until the eve of Good Friday, but instead he rode into the maenol in the afternoon of Palm Sunday, flung his reins to a groom, and came striding into the high chamber where Llewelyn was.

'My lord,' he said, hoarse with long riding and the dust of Spring, 'I pray your pardon but this cannot wait. The word that came into my hall this morning I've ridden to bring you as fast as I could. There's battle and slaughter broke loose at Hawarden! In the night a Welsh force has stormed and sacked the castle. Clifford is prisoner, and all his garrison killed or captive.'

AFTERGLOW AND NIGHTFALL

This was the lightning raid on the eve of Palm Sunday 1282, which began the war of 1282 and the final conquest of Wales. Llewelyn was kept in ignorance until it was a *fait accompli*, since David knew he would not willingly countenance an attack against the terms of the treaty he had accepted. But once the die was cast, he had no choice but to join his brother, and fight out to the end the last engagement in the tragedy of Wales.

Ewloe Castle

The site of Ewloe castle lies to the east of Offa's Dyke, and though it did change hands several times in the twelfth and thirteenth centuries, it was more often English than Welsh. It is possible that Owain Gwynedd built the first motte and bailey fortress on the site, about 1146, when he was expanding his holdings to the east, and captured Mold. Llewelyn the Great held Ewloe until his death, but during his son David's succession the English recovered much of north-east Wales, including this vulnerable outpost. Llewelyn ap Griffith recaptured it, and enlarged it by the addition of a curtain wall and the west tower. After the Edwardian conquest, and the building of Flint and Rhuddlan castles in their final form, Ewloe ceased to be of any strategic importance, and fell into disuse.

Dating from the twelfth century, Ewloe is one of the few Welsh-built castles remaining without English additions.

Flint Castle

In ten days they had cut their way to within a few miles of the abbey of Basingwerk, where there was a great level plane of rock jutting out into the estuary, and there the main army made a strong camp, cleared about on every side so that we had no cover to approach them undetected. And there they stayed, so arraying their forces that it was clear they meant to fortify and hold that spot as a base. This rock we called the Flint.

THE HOUNDS OF SUNSET

This was the beginning of the building of Flint Castle, during Edward I's Welsh war of 1277. The softening-up process had begun during the previous year, with *carte blanche* to all the barons of the March to attack and compress Welsh power wherever they could. In the summer of 1277 the king himself took the field with the feudal host and large companies of paid troops, pushing along the north coast from Chester and cutting wide roads through the forest before the army, to open up permanent approaches for the future. At Flint rapid fortifications were constructed, with a view to serious building later. Building in stone began as soon as Llewelyn ap Griffith accepted terms of peace in November 1277, and the work was pressed ahead rapidly, to be followed by the

The north-west keep of Flint Castle, overlooking the Dee Estuary.

founding of a defended town. Coastwise ships could then navigate the estuary of the Dee, so that a castle so placed could be victualled and relieved from the sea. From the land its situation was more vulnerable, but Edward ensured that the actual building should be virtually impregnable, even if the large outer bailey should be taken.

In the later war of 1282, when David raised the aggrieved Welsh again in revolt against the hated administration of the Crown, he seized the town of Flint, but wasted no time upon attempting the castle.

David, they said, was at Flint, and the town there was his, and the English, such as were in the town and not the castle, dead or captive. But the castle, being so placed on that great plain of rock jutting out into the estuary, was strongly held, and could be supplied by sea from Chester, and they doubted if any attempt would be made to take it, for since it could be isolated and passed by at will it was not worth the men it would cost in the assault, or, above all, the time, where time was more precious than gold. For in the surprise of this rising lay its best strength. So it was possible, they said, that David had left force enough to hold down Flint from the landward side, and himself rushed on to Rhuddlan.

AFTERGLOW AND NIGHTFALL

In the square inner bailey of Flint there were three corner towers, of which this is the most intact, and the fourth corner was filled by the enormous tower of the Donjon.

St Winifred's Well

This splendid group of buildings, terraced up a steep slope beside the road, just outside the town of Holywell, has been a place of pilgrimage ever since the first wooden commemorative chapel was built here by St Beuno in the seventh century, the continuity of worship here virtually unbroken in all those years, even when Catholics risked life and limb by practising their faith.

Lying just a few miles inland from the abbey of Basingwerk, the foundation of the well and its church became a bone of contention between Welsh and English for many years, just as a secular property might be fought over. In this case, after 1147, when Basingwerk, like all the Savignac monasteries, was absorbed into the Cistercian Order, the white monks claimed possession of the church of Holywell and the miraculous spring which rose from the virgin Winifred's blood, although in 1093 the Countess Adeliza of Chester had given the advowson and privileges to the Benedictines of St Werburgh's abbey of Chester. Eventually Basingwerk was in possession from 1240 until the Dissolution in 1537. Well before that date, probably in the latter half of the fifteenth century, the beautiful well chapel over the spring had been built, largely through the piety and generosity of Margaret, Countess of Richmond, Lady Margaret Beaufort, the mother of Henry VII, the first of the Tudor line. The crypt of the chapel roofs over and enshrines the spring, in a star-shaped enclosure of stone, and, in an unroofed level outside, the water fills a stone-lined pool for bathing. The building has suffered various changes during times of harsher measures against Catholics, but has been restored later to its proper form. No strictures, no persecutions, ever succeeded in preventing the faithful from reaching this place of pilgrimage. No

The tranquil garden by St Winifred's well at Holywell.

doubt in the worst days of religious intolerance many people, priests and worshippers died because of their determination to preserve the sanctity of the saint's memory.

Above this green garden on the lowest plane a path climbs to the porch of the enclosure which holds the pool, and beyond that lies the vaulted well chamber, cool, elegant, full of fine, exuberant but badly-weathered carving, as the frontage over the pool is open to the air. The chapel above the well chamber is entered from a higher level, and above all is the parish church. The entire group has a grace and harmony very grateful to the eye and the mind.

Basingwerk Abbey

It was our design to harry their every move by raids, and draw them as far into the forest as we could, where we could pick off any stragglers very easily, and hamper all their movements, especially since we expected them to be laden with all their baggage and supplies once they moved from Chester. And this was the first miscalculation, for they had now a large and powerful fleet lying in the estuary, and when they marched from Chester they marched as light as we, the ships carrying their supplies and keeping pace with them along the coast. Nor did Edward advance deep into the forest at all. He moved with method along the coast, his ships alongside, and all that great army of knights, troopers, archers and labourers went with him, north-westward towards the abbey of Basingwerk.

THE HOUNDS OF SUNSET

Basingwerk Abbey.

And there at Basingwerk, Edward established his personal head-quarters in the summer of 1277, while the building of Flint castle proceeded apace, and he paused to plan the next move in his campaign against Llewelyn. He even took time off to cross over and meet his queen in Cheshire, where they planned the foundation of a great new abbey at Vale Royal.

Basingwerk is an old site, inhabited during the Roman period, and possibly fortified in the heyday of the kings of Mercia. Offa's own son Cenwulf died there in the year 821, probably in arms against the Welsh. The abbey, founded in 1131 by Ranulf, Earl of Chester, was one of the fourteen houses of the Order of Savigny in Britain, but in the year 1147, after a long contention between the French houses of the order, who were pressing hard for the change, and the English monks, who put up a stout resistance, the entire order of Savigny was incorporated into Citeaux, and the monks were ordered to put off the grey habit and don the Cistercian white.

In return for the abbey's hospitality during the war of 1277 Edward granted it a number of privileges and favours. In later centuries the house had a reputation for lavish hospitality and rich living, before the last abbot ceded it to the Crown at the Dissolution, in 1516.

Rhuddlan Castle

The king's hall at Rhuddlan was a great structure of timber then, but the stone foundations of his new castle were already in, and the walls beginning to rise. Edward's knights were gathered to welcome the prince's party, squires came to hold his stirrup and take his bridle. The Earl of Lincoln and Bishop Burnell — for he was bishop of Bath and Wells as well as chancellor — ushered Llewelyn into the hall, and into Edward's presence, and the glitter of that military court, spare and deprived of the grace of women, made a fitting setting for the meeting of those two men. War was the business that had brought them together, war lost and won, and soldiers know the fickleness of victory and defeat, and the narrowness of the gap between them. A man does not mock what may be his own fate tomorrow, or a year hence, at least, no wise man.

THE HOUNDS OF SUNSET

This was on 10 November 1277, when the Treaty of Aberconwy was ratified, and king and prince met to confirm its acceptance. Llewelyn took the oath of fealty; the formal homage was delayed until they met again at Christmas in Westminster.

But the site of Rhuddlan had been of strategic importance from early days as both guarding and preserving the gateway into North Wales. It was the lowest point at which the River Clwyd could be forded, and from that ford a passable pathway ran on westward, through the widespread tidal marshes of the estuary. The Mercians made inroads there on two or three occasions; Offa's son is known to have died at Basingwerk. Shortly before the Norman invasion there was a fortified seat of the north Welsh princes there, a thorn in the English flesh, until Earl Harold seized and burned it. Some years later a Norman motte and bailey castle was installed there by the Norman Earl of Chester's deputy, who took the name of Robert of Rhuddlan.

For a century or more the site changed owners several times, as Welsh or Norman prevailed, and repeated castles, still in timber, were built, garrisoned, captured, burned, rebuilt and regarrisoned, and again destroyed. In the middle of the twelfth century they were still in timber, for there are records of expenditure on wood for repairs. Only with Edward I, by the time of his accession experienced in all manner of warfare, siege and defence, did the rebuilding assume the menacing durability of stone, and the design of castles develop towards the impregnable.

In the war of 1277 the king moved his headquarters forward to Rhuddlan, always the key to Snowdonia, where the castle must have been still habitable. He began work on his stone fortress at once. The actual site was slightly apart from Robert of Rhuddlan's motte and bailey. Edward was already employing as his architect James of St George, who was later responsible for all the great secondary wave castles of Edward's ambitious design to hold down Wales once and for all.

The south walls of the Edwardian
Rhuddlan Castle from the River
Clwyd.

Round his new castle Edward planted a new chartered borough,
inviting in English settlers at alluringly low rents, as at Flint and
later at Conwy, Caernarfon, Harlech and other places, and so
ensuring that the plantation should be defensible.

By the time of the second and final Welsh war Edward had also
taken care to make this advanced base, well into Welsh territory,
suppliable by sea, by canalizing the wandering River Clwyd into a
2-mile navigable channel, and draining the marshes of the former
delta. Henceforth sea-going ships could reach the castle dock, and
berth there. The river was tidal to a little above the castle, and thus
provided the inlet to the surrounding moat.

In the few subsequent Welsh risings, notably under Owen
Glendower, Rhuddlan was attacked, and the town ravaged, but the
castle was never taken. Even in its last military campaign, when it
was garrisoned for the king in the Civil War, it never fell to arms,
but after the Parliamentary victory was forced to surrender to

General Mytton. Parliament decreed that it should be slighted, and the damage clearly visible now was done to make it untenable for the future; thereafter, it was left to moulder, to be used as a convenient stone quarry, the usual fate of abandoned castles, and to silt up moat and tidal inlet and clothe its bare bones with bushes and trees, until it finally came into the hands of what was then the Ministry of Works, and began a respectful restoration to what it is today.

Chester

Chester, the Roman city and military base of Deva, has always been the key to north Wales, a centre of government, and the head of a region of palatine importance and independence. The Romans held it until withdrawal in 380, and left massive reminders of their long occupation.

What is now the cathedral site was originally a college of secular canons, dedicated to St Werburgh. The saint was not native here, but her relics were brought here in 875 by King Alfred's formidable daughter, Ethelfleda, the Lady of the Mercians, for safety from Danish attacks. Werburgh in her lifetime was Abbess of Ely, and died about the year 700. When the Normans came, and the Conqueror made Hugh d'Avranches Earl of Chester, with leave to add to his lands whatever he could win over the border in Wales, the earl refounded the college as a Benedictine monastery, and so it remained until the Dissolution, which happened here in 1541. Henry VIII then retained the great church, constantly enlarged and embellished since its Norman beginnings, with its claustral buildings complete, and created the new diocese of Chester, with the Benedictine abbey church as its cathedral. The title 'Bishop of Chester' is found much earlier in documents, but the diocese actually begins with Henry VIII's enactments. The ancient see of Mercia, based first and most frequently in Lichfield, was transferred for some years to Chester in the eleventh century, and to Coventry for a while in the twelfth, so that the titles of bishop attach in documents to any of the three cities during that period, and are sometimes used for both Coventry and Lichfield indiscriminately, at virtually the same date.

The Chester of the first Norman earls was almost an independent

Eastgate Street, Chester, looking west from the Eastgate parapet.

kingdom, with its own administration, exchequer, and *carte blanche* to add to its territory westward, as Earl Hugh proceeded to do. It was always one of the bases from which the feudal host, if used by the Crown, marched to the subjugation of Wales; though the feudal host, until augmented by the paid mercenaries preferred by Edward I in his version of total war, often proved ineffective, slow and clumsy against the light and rapid Welsh, and with the weather as their ally over the bleak hills, the Welsh irregulars could bog down kings in helpless chaos, and send them back home empty-handed. In serious warfare, however, Chester was immensely valuable because it was also a navigable port, and the English could bring round a fleet from the Cinque Ports into the city, and victual the northern castles from the sea. Not until the fifteenth century did the Dee silt up and render the estuary too dangerous and difficult for shipping.

After the death in 1232 of Earl Ranulf III de Blundeville, one of the finest characters of his time, generous and just even to his enemies and not afraid to reprove kings, and the subsequent death five years later of his only direct male heir, John the Scot, the succession was left in disorder among a number of heiresses of two generations, and the king bought out all their rights in Chester and the title, and took it into his own hands. In 1254 city, county and title were made a part of the lavish settlement on the Lord Edward, later Edward I, on the occasion of his marriage. During the brief period when Simon de Montfort was virtually ruling the country, though in the king's name, Simon gained possession of Chester by exchanging for it lands to the same value in less vulnerable places, but after the battle of Evesham Edward regained his earldom, and it has been regarded since as one of the traditional appanages of the heir to the throne.

It was to Chester that Richard II was lured from his refuge in Conwy, to meet with Bolingbroke, under oath that his royal right should not be challenged, only to be imprisoned and forced into abdication in favour of his cousin. It is recorded that it was the Earl of Northumberland who swore that Richard's sovereignty would be respected, but there is no way of knowing whether this was deliberate deception, or whether Northumberland himself had been deceived by Bolingbroke, or, indeed, whether events careered out of control by their own momentum, far beyond what Bolingbroke had originally intended. They ended in the usurpation of Henry IV, and the death of Richard.

RIGHT

Thirteenth-century vaulting in the cloister of Chester Cathedral.

Note on Access

Welsh Historic Monuments (Cadw):
(Opening times: daily in the summer; between 9.30 a.m. and
4 p.m. weekdays and 2 p.m. and 4 p.m. on Sundays in the winter.)

Chepstow Castle, Tintern Abbey, Raglan Castle, Abergavenny
Castle, Tretower Castle and Court, Montgomery Castle, Strata
Marcella, Valle Crucis, Denbigh Castle, Rhuddlan Castle.

Grosmont Castle, Skenfrith Castle, White Castle, Dinas Bran
Castle, The Castle of Hope, Ewloe Castle, Flint Castle and
Basingstoke Abbey are also in the keeping of Cadw and are open at
any reasonable time.

English Heritage:
(Opening times: daily between 10 a.m. and 4 p.m. from Easter
until the end of September; between 10 a.m. and 4 p.m. Tuesday –
Sunday during the winter.)

Stokesay Castle, Clun Castle (currently under repair), and Much
Wenlock Priory.

Longtown Castle, Wigmore Castle, Moreton Corbet and Acton
Burnell – also English Heritage sites – are open throughout the
year.

National Trust:
Powis Castle (Welshpool) is open on Sunday afternoons throughout the winter and daily (except Mondays and Tuesdays) during the
summer. Chirk Castle is open daily except Monday and Saturday
throughout the summer.

Others

Hawarden Castle is in private ownership and can be visited on Sunday afternoons during the summer.

Abbey Cwm Hir, Cefnllys, Richard's Castle and Arthur's Stone are on open land and can be visited at any time.

Most of the churches and cathedrals are open to the public during the hours of daylight throughout the year.

Please note that at the present time English Heritage is discussing the dispersion of its properties, and access conditions may change in the future. As the National Trust may change its visiting times from year to year, the above information is also subject to change.

Index

Illustrations are shown in italic.